Amigurumi
Animals

Amigurumi Animals

15 patterns and dozens of techniques for creating cute crochet creatures

Annie Obaachan

St. Martin's Griffin
New York

This edition published by St. Martin's Press 2008.

www.stmartins.com

A Quintet Book. Copyright © 2008 Quintet Publishing Limited. All rights reserved.

This book was designed and produced by
Quintet Publishing Limited, 6 Blundell Street, London N7 9BH, UK

Art Director: Sofia Henry
Designer: Jason Anscomb
Photography: Lizzie Orme
Illustrator: Bernard Chau
Project Editor: Katy Bevan
Managing Editor: Donna Gregory
Publisher: Gillian Laskier

Printed in China

Library of Congress Cataloging-in-Publication Data Available Upon Request

ISBN-13: 978-0-312-37820-2
ISBN-10: 0-312-37820-3

First U.S. Edition: February 2008

10 9 8 7 6 5 4 3 2 1

Contents

Foreword	6
What is amigurumi?	8
Japanese dolls	12
Amigurumi	**page 14**
Making crochet dolls	16
Materials	18
Reading patterns	20
Crochet techniques	22
Design your own	**page 30**
Designing animals from sketches	32
Making shapes with circular crochet	36
Finishing touches	38
The menagerie	**page 44**
Pig	46
Cheeky bunny	50
Penguins	54
Bear	58
Grumpy tiny mohair bear	62
Tanuki	66
Lion	70
Magpies	74
Sausage dog	78
Owl	82
Monkey	86
Panda bear	90
Field mouse	94
Skinny sleepy cat	96
Elephant	100
Amigurumi gallery	**page 104**
Resources	124
Index	126

Foreword

My mother taught me to crochet when I was quite small. I failed the first time round and didn't enjoy it, but when I started again as a teenager it all came back to me. I remember well the crochet bikini I made out of fluorescent-pink-itchy yarn.

In Japan the third of March is the Doll's Festival. Each family has a set of dolls that were bought, or handed down the generations. When I was born my grandmother bought a set for me, to celebrate being the first girl born to the family. I had a collection of regular children's dolls as well—Snoopy, giant bears, and the like. I also had some kokeshi dolls as souvenirs from different parts of the country—although the stories we learned about them still give me goose bumps as kokeshi means, "disappeared child." A long time ago when Japan was a rural community, farmers in the countryside were often struggling. People had to sell or sacrifice their children to give their spirits to their god, so the wooden kokeshi dolls were a child-replacement.

I studied fashion design at the Bunka Fashion College, Tokyo. There I learned skills from pattern cutting and sewing to merchandising. Then later I worked for the costume studio at Disneyland making life-sized outfits. I made a flesh-colored body suit with muscle textures for a sailor, and plenty of mermaids' tails, that kind of silly thing.

Annie Obaachan

(Grannie Annie)

I was dreaming about coming to London, and saving money for the trip. When I finally got to London I met Rosie and Harriet from Tatty Devine. They introduced me to Rachael Matthews and the Cast Off knitting group. I then helped Rachael with Cast Off, working on her books *Knitorama* and *Hookorama*, before helping with her exhibition in 2006.

I love to crochet anything. My ambition is to make a range of crocheted-popcorn jewelry... coming soon!

What is amigurumi?

You can use your whole mouth to form the word, in a variety of different voices... Aa-miii-gaa-ruu-miii. The word has so many vowel sounds, that you can pull up to five funny faces just in the process of saying it. Once you have practiced saying "amigurumi" in an animated manner, and learned the basics of crochet, you have probably grasped the concept of this book. You are about to launch yourself into a cartoon world, where any mood is acceptable.

Amigurumi is a recently coined word. "Ami" means knit in Japanese, and "nuigurumi" means stuffed creature—so knit it, stuff it, and you have amigurumi. These are anthropomorphic creatures that you are giving life to—you could never make the same one twice, as each one is unique.

Japan has a rich history of textiles, especially in the art of kimonos, where you find beautifully crafted *ikat-kasuri* weaving, batik, *shibori*, wood-block printing, to name but a few—but no knitting. Knitting and crochet are not indigenous to Japan. The samurai warriors took up knitting to make socks with toes that allowed more freedom of motion, but for a long time, they were the only ones forming knitting circles.

In the West, we have no history of amigurumi as we see it in this book. We talk about yarn, and immediately think of functional items, like cardigans, sweaters, socks, and gloves. Traditionally, we knit or crochet from patterns, typed in an abbreviated language, which instructs us to make shapes that we join, and fashion around our bodies. Without a picture of one that's been made earlier, when we read our patterns, we can only imagine the finished result.

The Japanese, with no prior knitting tradition, invented a new use for knitting and crochet in their culture and a new way of writing patterns. Amigurumi seems to have grown naturally with the way the charts developed. Pictures are drawn with crochet and sometimes the images become little creatures. Japanese writing comprises pictures and symbols, and knitting and crochet stitches are represented in the same way. Throughout this book, you will see beautifully drawn charts. Don't feel you have to "read" every stitch. Charts are designed as a full picture of how a pattern is expected to evolve. They show you where you are heading. Let your eyes roll around and around the spiraled paths and kaleidoscopic circles, and they will take you on a rhythmic journey toward finding a new friend. Meditating in circles and lines gives us plenty of time to conjure up extraordinary personae. The Japanese would never waste time telling you how to knit. They assume that you know the basics, and expect you to dive in and make whatever comes naturally.

So why do we want to make little stuffed crochet creatures in the first place? They may be very small and cute, but they have weighty cultural significance. Type amigurumi in a search engine, and they are everywhere, millions of them, and some of them are real enough to write their own blogs. Amigurumi as a phenomenon has been growing slowly since the 1950s. It was at this time that Japanese culture moved toward cuteness, or *kawaii*, inventing characters like Hello Kitty, a cute white kitten with a little bow on one ear, who could be happy or sad, but we're not sure which because she has no mouth and just stares. At the end of World War II, atom bombs were dropped on Hiroshima and Nagasaki. Japan lost its political strength, and its ancient culture, leaving behind a country like a lost child, to be re-born, and re-formed with a deliberate avoidance of what had happened before. It was not possible to think about what had happened. A new culture of "cuteness" served as a mask for all the atrocities.

During the 1960s, the Japanese government encouraged economic expansion over cultural preservation, dissolving communities and regionally distinct traditions. Families moved to big cities to find jobs. Little Hello Kitty and her other nu-cultural friends were developed as mass marketable icons, spreading a cute, pacifying force over a new nation of "salary men" and "office ladies." These were white-collar workers, who turned Japan around into an economic power. These slaves to the wage, with long working hours and a low prestige in the corporate hierarchy, were the workers that helped develop technology we now use worldwide. Another new word was born—*karoshi*—meaning death from overwork.

Most of us have a friend, or are ourselves, an absentee who is devoted to their work and missing out on the rest of life. A typical modern job might demand the wearing of a uniform, and the conducting of friendships through text messaging and email, which unfortunately means we can't use all the little noises, faces, and gestures we normally use to express ourselves. Amigurumi step into the breach. They offer us cute individual characters formed by human hands. The materials are chosen with love and care. The pacifying force is still there but it's heavily personalized. They are sweet gestures, with no particular depth of message, but characters with very colorful, anthropological histories, which are a light relief in a time when collective joy and culture can be of second importance.

There might be someone over there, sitting at their desk, on the end of a mass of electrical connections, whose life would be greatly enriched by a couple of fire-fighter pigs, which don't quite look like the ones demonstrated on page 46 of this book, because you made them yourself and they have become their own characters. In addition, if you are one of those workers who is an integral part of a larger machine, and you never see the product of what your company makes, then crafting an amigurumi superhero panda to decorate your office is a fast route to satisfaction. On the other hand, maybe something shocked you and you don't know what to say or do. You might need space to organize your thoughts, but in the meantime, making little magpies sitting on a washing line might make you feel better.

We are free to go forth and crochet. You can grunt, growl, or make cute little baby noises while your hands are working on the lovely projects in the pages that follow. As the faces start to emerge and smile back, you are in this together. Soon you will find a completely new species staring back at you, asking you to join them.

Rachael Matthews

Japanese dolls

There is a long history of doll making in Japan, which runs parallel to the culture of giving gifts, or *omiyage*. Giving gifts at every opportunity, to a new co-worker, neighbor, or just as a token of friendship, is a way of life in Japan. Dolls from different regions became suitable gifts or souvenirs for bringing home after a trip, as symbols of purity or as good luck charms.

Kokeshi are traditional dolls originating from northern Japan. They have no arms or legs, just a simple torso and oversized head. Usually carved in wood, the designs vary depending on the region. Dolls that are more creative, with expressions and fashionable dress, are now in vogue. **Momiji** dolls are a modern version of these gifts of friendship, which have a hole in the base where you can insert a small note to the recipient, and have become collectible items.

Daruma dolls are representations of a Buddhist priest, Bodhidharma. The dolls have no arms and legs, resembling a large head. They are usually made of papier-mâché and painted red. Given as gifts at New Year, you paint in one eye to represent making a resolution, then, when the challenge is achieved, you can paint in the other. These days they are available to bulk-buy as corporate gifts.

Okiagari-koboshi are much like the daruma dolls, but blue and white. They too represent a priest, and have a rotund shape. The weighted base means that they bounce back upright when knocked down, like a child's toy. They symbolize the resilience needed to bounce back from the challenges that life throws at us.

Hakata dolls are carved from clay, then a mold is made to cast a finer doll. It is thought that hakata were originated by a master tile-maker working to build Fukuoka Castle in the seventeenth century. Pottery became fashionable and the dolls' popularity spread across the country.

Hina Matsuri, or the Doll's Festival, is celebrated in the spring. Traditionally set adrift in a river, these beautiful handmade dolls now tend to be saved, and collected from one year to the next. Originally made from a clay-like sawdust paste, and painted with powdered seashell and animal glue (*gofun*), they were dressed in traditional costumes. Bought now, they are more likely to be mass-produced.

Traditional Japanese dolls are collector's items. Left: these wooden kokeshi in Sakunami-style are from the Sendai area. Right: a daruma stares blankly, waiting for his eyes to be painted in.

Amigurumi

Making crochet dolls

Crafted with circular crochet, amigurumi differ only slightly from other crocheted items. They are often worked in spirals, rather than in steps—if you wanted to keep stripes level, without creating a step, you would make an elevating chain at the beginning of each row. Spirals are much easier, as you just keep on going without even linking the rows with a slip stitch. This will be easier for newcomers, as anyone who has been doing crochet for a while will be stuck with the turning-chain habit. You can use either technique with the patterns in this book.

Made using a hook slightly smaller than you would normally use for the weight of yarn, amigurumi can have a very tight gauge. This is good, as the stuffing will not fall out through any holes in the firm fabric. Experiment using different yarns. Fluffy mohair and alpaca yarns are ideal for some of the more hairy creatures, as well as being comforting and soft to hold. Acrylic and woolen yarns have good elasticity, while pure cotton yarns will help you to keep a tight gauge as it has very little "give."

For stuffing your creations, the material that you use depends on the size of the creature, the desired effect, and most importantly, what you have on hand. Toy stuffing like Poly-fil, or cotton batting, is probably the most used item. However, if you don't have any, and you are in a hurry, you can cut up old, or tattered hosiery. If the critter is really tiny, you may be able to make do with scraps of yarn.

Plastic pellets are useful for keeping the bottom of the shape heavy, making your figure more stable and able to stand up easily. Use pellets in the bottom half of the stuffing, in the feet or tail, then continue with soft stuffing for the rest of the body. Stuffing completely with pellets will create a bean bag effect, where the beans move around the body.

HOW TO READ A CHART

In Japan, they just use charts. This is also true in continental European countries like France and Spain. In the USA, and the traditional UK, we like to have it written out. So, for those of you not used to using a chart, prepare to be amazed. It makes the whole thing much easier. You can visualize the shape you are going to make before it happens, which seems, logically, to be a better way to get the information into your brain and out through your hands.

These charts are simplicity itself, as they mostly use only one type of stitch. Follow a circular chart from the center. The loops will indicate the beginning of each row, so you can keep count (it may be useful to use a stitch marker, or ring of scrap yarn as well). Each X is a single crochet stitch, and where there is an arrow, it means that this is an increase or decrease, depending on which way the arrow is pointing. It should be obvious; if you are getting bigger, it means increasing. The charts change to straight lines to show the shape getting smaller again—then the decreases are easier to see. (See the symbol chart on page 29.)

Materials

HOOKS

Crochet hooks come in all shapes and sizes. In fact, even some that are the same size will say something different on them, just to confuse you. The US has its own system. In Europe, the sizes are measured in millimeters.

There are also traditional sizing systems in the UK, Canada, and Japan, so if you inherit vintage hooks you should size them with a gauge, or check the conversion charts on page 21. Carved from wood, bone, or ivory, older hooks sometimes have hooks at both ends. You can find some early Bakelite and resin hooks in antique stores, although they are increasingly sought after by collectors.

Used for the finest crochet work, fine steel hooks or pins work well with shiny, mercerized cotton or silks. Chunky and novelty yarns can be worked with giant plastic hooks. Hooks made of the finest woods, or bamboo, are beautiful to handle, although many hookers prefer the speed of an aluminum hook with a soft and ergonomic grip.

YARNS

You can crochet with any kind of long thread, but the best results are often obtained with smooth, well-spun yarns. Any yarn that could split, will split when you try to crochet with it. The joy of making small things is that you get to use up all those scraps of yarn that have been left over from other projects. We don't specify the brands of yarn used in this book. Some of them were scraps from the bottom of a workbox, others were expensive alpacas. The point is you can use what you have, thus making your critters unique, as well as saving pennies.

Best kept tied to your workbasket: sharp scissors for cutting yarn and trimming ends.

Knitters' pins with large heads are useful for pinning together shapes.

You'll need a blunt-ended needle for sewing up seams and threading in ends. [as above]

Split stitch markers are good for crochet, so that you can mark the beginning of each round.

A tape measure is good to check the gauge, if you have been given one, or if you want to repeat a shape in different yarns.

Reading patterns

Looking at a crochet pattern for the first time must feel like reading another language. The shortened words are there to prevent laborious repetition and to make the patterns shorter and easier to follow. If in doubt, look at the abbreviations chart below to clarify what is meant.

CROCHET ABBREVIATIONS	
*	repeat instructions between asterisks as many times as directed or repeat from a given set of instructions
alt	alternate
approx	approximately
beg	begin/beginning
bet	between
ch	chain stitch
cm	centimeter(s)
col	color
cont	continue
dc	double crochet
dec	decrease/decreases/decreasing
foll	follow/follows/following
inc	increase/increases/increasing
mm	millimeter(s)
rep	repeat(s)
rnd(s)	round(s)
RS	right side
sc	single crochet
sc2tog	single crochet 2 stitches together
sk	skip
Sl st	slip stitch
sp(s)	space(s)
st(s)	stitch(es)
tog	together
tr	treble crochet
yoh	yarn over hook

UK CROCHET TERMS ARE DIFFERENT		
US	**UK**	
Sl st	ss	slip stitch
ch	ch	chain
sc	dc	US single crochet = UK double crochet
dc	tr	US double crochet = UK treble crochet
tr	dtr	US treble crochet = UK double treble crochet
dtr	trtr	US double treble crochet = UK triple treble crochet

Welcome to the kooky world of hook sizes. The letters and numbers may vary, so if in doubt, and you probably will be, the metric sizes are the only ones that you can check with a tape measure. Your knitting needle gauge will also work for the metric sizes so you can convert those lovely vintage patterns. Beware though, Japanese hook sizes are different again. They start off looking similar to the American sizes, then vary, then after 7mm they revert to the metric system. Good luck!

USA	Metric	Old UK	Japanese
	2 mm	14	0
B-1	2.25 mm		
	2.5 mm	12	1 (2.4 mm)
C-2	2.75 mm		2 (2.7 mm)
	3 mm	11	3
D-3	3.25 mm	10	4 (3.4 mm)
E-4	3.5 mm	9	5 (3.6 mm)
F-5	3.75 mm		6 (3.9 mm)
G-6	4 mm	8	7 (4.2 mm)
7	4.5 mm	7	8
H-8	5 mm	6	9 (4.8 mm)
			10 (5.1 mm)
I-9	5.5 mm	5	11 (5.4 mm)
J-10	6 mm	4	13
K-10½	6.5 mm	3	14 (6.3 mm)
			15 (6.6 mm)
	7 mm	2	7 mm
L-11	8 mm	0	8 mm
M/N-13	9 mm	00	9 mm
N/P-15	10 mm	000	10 mm
	12 mm		
P/Q	15 mm		

Crochet techniques

The basics of crochet are very simple. Once you have made a basic chain you are well on your way, as even the most complicated and decorative stitches are just variations on this simple stitch. These instructions are for a right-handed person. If you are left-handed, look at the step images in a mirror and they will show you the correct way to do the stitch.

Holding the hook and yarn

There are many individual ways of holding the hook and yarn in crochet and it may feel awkward at first. Here are just two examples—choose whichever variation seems to come naturally to you.

1. Hold the hook in your right hand as you would a knife.
2. Hold the hook in your right hand as you would a pencil.

Wrap the ball end of the yarn around the little finger of your left hand, passing it under the third or middle finger and over your forefinger, using the forefinger to create tension. OR Wrap the ball end of the yarn around the little finger of your left hand, passing it over the middle finger. Hold the work steady with your thumb and forefinger, using the middle finger to create tension.

Holding the hook and yarn

Holding the hook like a knife

Holding the hook like a pencil

Holding the yarn

Make a slipknot

Make a loop in the yarn. With your crochet hook catch the ball end of the yarn and draw through loop. Pull firmly on yarn and hook to tighten knot to create your first loop.

Slipknot

Making a chain

Making a chain

1. To make a chain, hold the tail end of yarn with the left hand and bring the yarn over hook (yoh) by passing hook in front of the yarn, under and around it.
2. Keeping the tension in the yarn taut, draw the hook and yarn through the loop.
3. Pull the yarn and hook through the hole and begin again, ensuring that the stitches are fairly loose. Repeat to make the number of chain required. As the chain lengthens keep hold of the bottom edge to maintain the tension.

How to count a chain

To count the stitches, use the right side of the chain, or the side that has more visible and less twisted "V" shapes, as shown. Don't count the original slip stitch, but count each "V" as one chain.

Count a chain

Make a slip stitch (Sl st)

A slip stitch is used to join one stitch to another or a stitch to another point, as in joining a circle, and is usually made by picking up two strands of a stitch. However, where it is worked into the starting chain only pick up the back loop.

1. Insert the hook into the back loop of the next stitch and pass yarn over hook (yoh), as in chain stitch.
2. Draw yarn through both loops on stitch and repeat.

Working in the round

There are two ways to begin circular crochet—with a chain or a loop. Also known as a magic ring, or finger loop, a loop is the more usual way to make amigurumi. This way of working in the round ensures that there is no hole in the middle of the work, as there is with a chain ring, as the central hole is adjustable and can be pulled tightly closed.

Making a magic ring
1. Make a loop with tail end of yarn on right, ball end on left.
2. Pull ball end through loop (you will need to steady work with hand).
3. Make one chain through loop on hook you have drawn through to steady the round.
4. Work as many sc, or whatever stitch you are using, into the loop as is required by pattern.
5. Pull the ends of yarn tight to draw in circle, so you have no hole in the middle of first round.

Making a magic ring

Making a chain ring

Making a chain ring
1. Work a chain as long as required by pattern.
2. Join last chain to first with a slip stitch. Begin first round by working into each chain stitch.

Single crochet (sc)

This is the main stitch that is used in amigurumi.

1. Insert hook, front to back into next stitch, two strands and one loop on hook. Yoh.
2. Draw through one loop to front, there should be two loops on hook. Yoh.
3. Draw through both loops to complete single crochet. Work one sc into every stitch to end of round.

Single crochet

1

2

3

Double crochet (dc)

This makes a more open fabric. The stitch is called a treble in the UK because of the three moves to make the stitch.

1. Wrap the yarn over the hook (yoh) from back to front. Insert hook into next stitch, from front to back. Yoh again and draw through stitch.
2. There should be three loops on hook. Yoh and pull through two loops. Two loops on hook. Yoh. Pull through remaining two loops to complete.

Half-double crochet
The half-double is just that, half a double crochet. In step 2, pull through all the remaining loops in one movement.

Double crochet

Half double

Treble crochet (tr)

This elongated stitch is only used once in the wings of the magpies, so you don't have to worry about it until page 76.

1. Wrap yarn round hook twice (yoh twice). Insert hook into next stitch, yoh again.
2. Pull yarn through stitch to front, there should be four loops on hook, yoh. Draw yarn through two loops, leaving three loops on hook.
3. Yoh. Draw yarn through two loops, leaving two loops on hook, yoh.
4. Pull yarn through both remaining loops to complete treble.

Treble crochet

Putting it all together

Finishing is a very important part of crochet as it could make or break your project. The perfect join should be one you can't distinguish from the work, as bad finishing is always noticeable and messy. Luckily, most of your finishing points will be hidden in the joints of the animal, so often there is no need to even close the shape completely.

1. When you finish off the end of your arm, or leg, keep a long yarn end for sewing in, then when you are attaching the limb to the body you will be using the same color.

2. Hold the two pieces to be connected together in your left hand, or in your right if you are left-handed. With the left-over yarn and a blunt tapestry needle sew the two pieces together with a whipstitch. Take the needle into the main body, and bring the needle back up inside the edge of the new limb. Continue all the way around.

3. As the yarn is the same color, the stitches will be almost invisible. Piece the sections together as shown in your assembly diagram.

Sewing two pieces together

Fastening off

1. After finishing the last stitch, snip off yarn from ball, leaving a couple of inches to weave in. Yoh.
2. Draw through tail, pulling tightly to fasten.

Weaving in ends

1. Use hook to draw yarn through at least five stitches, winding the yarn over and under as you go to secure yarn and ensure it doesn't work free.
2. Snip off excess yarn.

Slip stitch join

Place two pieces together, right sides facing. Work a row of slip stitch along the join, inserting needle through back loops only of both pieces (the two loops which touch when placed side by side).

Single crochet join

Place two pieces together, right sides facing. Work a row of sc along the join of the two pieces, going through the whole of both stitches.

Whipstitch

Place two pieces together, and using a knitter's needle, join the back loops of each piece with a diagonal stitch motion. Use this stitch when attaching patches of felt, or other fabric, for faces or clothing.

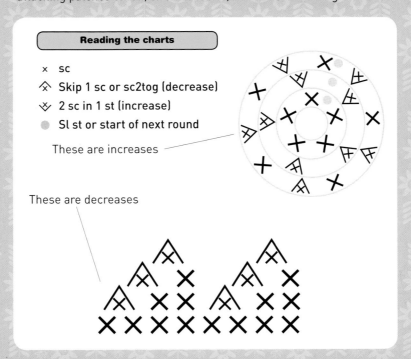

Reading the charts

× sc

⤅ Skip 1 sc or sc2tog (decrease)

⤋ 2 sc in 1 st (increase)

● Sl st or start of next round

These are increases

These are decreases

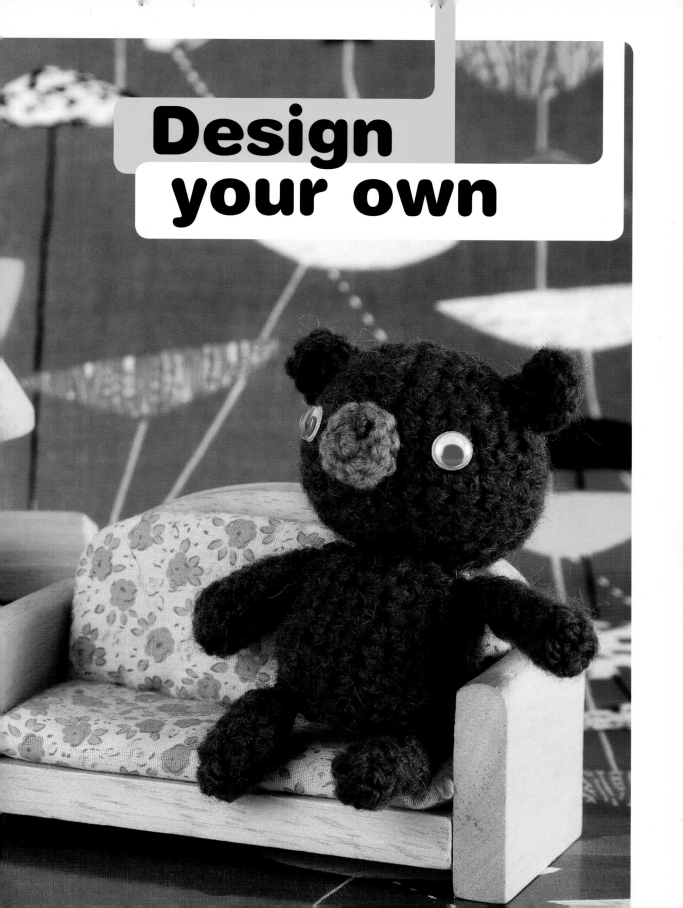

Design
your own

Designing animals from sketches

You may be able to picture something in your imagination, but it is often only when consigning it to paper that it really begins to emerge and develop. You may notice inconsistencies in your original plan, and be able to correct them, before proceeding with any work. Patterns and shapes may emerge that were not obvious before. It is difficult for any mind to put together three-dimensional shapes without drawing them out first, and since most handicraft takes some time, it is best not to waste yours by not planning thoroughly. Don't be put off if you feel you are not a natural artist. Sketches are just that, sketchy: they are simply a tool, not the final product.

Take your inspiration from nature, sketching your pets, animals in a field, or at a zoo. If working from the real thing is not an option, use photographs of animals (either your own, or from books and magazines). Use your sketching to simplify the shapes of the animal's body—perhaps the body is egg-shaped, while the head is more spherical. Once you start looking closely, you'll realize that all animals are made up of the same simple sphere, egg, cylinder, or triangular shapes. You can crochet modules of different shapes and sizes (see page 36).

Consider whether your creature is on all fours, of if it will sit, or stand up. Take balance into account when considering proportions—a huge head will find it hard to balance on a tiny body and legs, and likewise a tiny head will get lost on a large frame. Thinking about shape also allows you to consider which technique would be most suitable to create the effect that you need. A curled edge or striped body, for instance, may need a particular stitch.

TIP
Experimenting with different yarn weights and fibers will help you create amigurumi with an exciting range of textures, even though you only use the single crochet stitch.

Rabbit - different types of yarn.

Shape = sphere.

tucked in →

Felt yarn → mohair.

coil?

Rabbit
The arms and legs changed
from the original sketch
to the final version, as they
were too small.

Tanuki (racoon dog). two colours crocheting.

dark orange.
yellow.

different way
of making BODY
2 parts Front / Back

Felt
eye

Tanuki
This is a more complicated
design, with color changes
to consider, alongside
the shapes.

Extra
semi sphere
for tummy

Stripy crochet

Face expression

Cheeky bunny
This rabbit was born with a cheeky expression.

Decorative details
It is at this stage that you can try out decorative touches, without putting in too much effort.

Gift box
This is designed to hide a ring inside an animal's body.

Satin St embroider

Bear symmetry
Animals are usually symmetrical, so it makes sense to draw them that way. That makes it clear what you need two of.

Simplified body
This shape ended up on the lion. Extreme simplification can be effective.

Headdress
This design uses the bear attached to a hat for some groovy headgear.

Owl evolution
This lovely nocturnal creature is actually quite a complicated group of shapes.

Simplified owl
This is a simplified version of the original owl drawing.

Final shape
This is the final shape, where the whole bird is reduced to one main shape, and the eyes have become exaggerated.

Lion's mane
The lion's mane becomes his distinguishing feature.

Making shapes with circular crochet

When you've had a little experience of making amigurumi creatures, it's easy to create your own designs. Great drawing skills and knowledge of animal anatomy are not required. Working from photographic reference, heads can be simplified to spheres, bodies become simple egg shapes, and arms and legs are sausages. Look at the proportions of the animal and exaggerate these to create stylized amigurumi creatures. The majority of amigurumi seem to have distorted proportions, part of their _kawaii_ appeal. They have oversized heads and large doleful eyes.

Working in rounds, as opposed to rows, means the work continues as such, with no turning. This means it is easy to lose which row you are on and stitch markers are a good idea to remind you of where you started. Either you work in spirals, or the last stitch of each round is joined by a slip stitch to the first stitch, it doesn't matter which you choose (see page 16).

FLAT DISC
To create a flat circle, rather than a tube, you will need to increase in every row. Work two stitches into each stitch in the first row, then into every other stitch in the following row, every third stitch in the third row, and so on, until you reach the diameter you require.

SPHERE
To make a three-dimensional round shape you will need to increase the diameter, then level off briefly before beginning to decrease. Work two stitches into each stitch in the first row, then every other stitch in the following row, every third stitch in the third row. Keep straight for one round before beginning to reduce stitches. Do this by working two stitches together every alternate stitch in the following row, and every third stitch in the next row, and so on.

TO JOIN IN NEW YARN
When the yarn runs out, or you want to change color, change yarns carefully, in order to prevent making a hole. Fasten off first color and make a slipknot on your hook. Insert hook from front to back in stitch where you wish to begin new color. Draw the hook through to front. Insert the hook into next stitch and work the stitch required by your pattern.

EGG SHAPE

To make the fat end of the egg, increase in every stitch in the first row, every alternate stitch in the second row, every third stitch in the third row, every forth stitch in the forth row. Keep straight for one round, then begin decreasing gradually as before, but with a straight row between each decrease row (as used in the Penguin pattern).

SAUSAGE

This is similar to making a sphere. After the initial increasing rows keep straight for the required length, then begin decreasing rows as before.

HALF SPHERE

Make this just like the sphere, but fasten off at the halfway point.

SQUARES

It can be done, but not in rounds. Don't bother, as there aren't many animals that need cubes.

Finishing touches

Embroidery is an effective way of adding interest to your projects and complements the texture of crochet. Here are some simple stitches that you may like to try. It may help to use a blunt knitter's needle, as this will not split the yarn as embroidery needles do, and will slip through the crochet stitches easily.

CHAIN STITCH

Insert needle from back to front of work and loop the thread back into same hole from front to back. Catch the loop with the point of the needle to create a chain. This is a useful stitch for curved shapes like flowers, or for handwriting script.

BLANKET STITCH

This stitch creates a neat edge, and is useful for straightening an uneven selvedge. Working along the edge, secure yarn at the back of work, insert the needle from front to back, with needle coming out of work in front of loop made by yarn. Pull needle through, tightening yarn against edge of work, repeat for length of edge.

SATIN STITCH

Work stitches closely together along the shape of the pattern you wish to make, keeping edges of shape even. This is most commonly used as a filler for eyes and other solid shapes.

OTHER EMBELLISHMENTS

Plastic eyes can give a fun look to your creations. They are available in all sorts of sizes from regular craft stores or on the Internet. There are even people out there who are making their own design of eyes specially for the growing amigurumi market. When you have your correct choice of eye and the critter is near completion, glue them on with wood glue. Some novelty yarns may resist the use of glue, so you will have to try another approach.

Felt or fabric can be used to emphasize eyes, cheeks, noses, and other facial features. Craft felt is a favorite, as it doesn't fray, so you can cut any shape, and glue or stitch it on. The field mouse on page 94 has the softest felt ears. Cut the felt to shape, then stitch around using a plain or decorative stitch. Blanket stitch would work well here.

Chain stitch

Blanket stitch

Satin stitch

Use whipstitch
or blanket stitch
to sew
on patches.

Sewing on felt

Circle
Start with a circle shape for the face and divide into quarters.

Muzzle
The nose and mouth are often connected in animal faces.

Cheeky
Try out alternative cheek positions for different looks.

Facial expressions

It is the faces of these creatures that give them such a human look, and you can change the way they look—lively or sleepy, happy or sad—with just a few lines. Look at the sketches for facial ideas to see how a simple line, or accent, can change a whole character.

It is automatic for us to draw the eyes in the top half of the face. In actual fact, for a human face, they should be placed at the halfway point between the chin and the top of the head. Divide your head into quarters. Try placing the nose on the central point, or below this line. Adding exaggerated anatomical features will help your creation to be recognizable: try a muzzle, or large ears, for instance.

This lion looks pretty serious. Turning up the corners of his mouth is easy, but try not to make him look foolish.

Eyelids
Droopy eyelids can look sad or tired, depending on how you draw them.

Cross-eyed
Make sure both eyes are looking in the same direction.

Eye, eye, Captain!

Making the eyes

When you look at someone's eyes, you will notice that you don't normally see the whole of the colored part of the eye, or iris. If you draw an eye like this, it creates a very "open-eyed" effect that is almost cartoonish—ideal, perhaps, for our little amigurumi.

You'll be surprised at what a difference you can make to an expression just with the eyes. Drooping eyelids, or heavy brows, will create a world-weary look. For large and lovable eyes, make the outside large, in embroidery or with felt, and add long lashes.

Have a look at some of your favorite cartoon characters for some good ideas. Use different colors at will, but it is best to maintain the contrast between the inner and outer eye: the whites of the eye look good in white or a pale shade. Raised eyebrows will also create a certain look.

Attach bought plastic eyes with glue, unless you are around small children, when they may not be safe. Fabric, embroidery, or crochet are all great alternatives.

All in favor say eye!

The eyes have it!

The menagerie

Pig

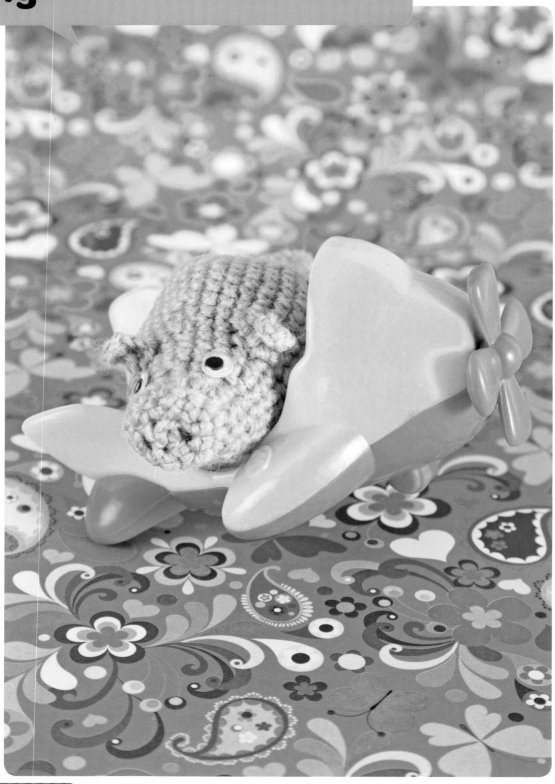

MATERIALS

C-2 (2.75 mm) hook
Pink yarn
Plastic eyes ¼ in. (7 mm) diameter

MEASUREMENTS

2¾ in. (7 cm) tall when piggybacked (one on top of the other)

DIRECTIONS

BODY

Make a loop with tail end of yarn on right, keeping ball end on left. Pull the ball end through loop. Make one chain through loop on hook you have drawn through to steady the circle. Sc 5 into the circle and complete with Sl st into the first sc.

Rnd 1: Sc 2 into each of 5 sc.
Rnd 2: * Sc 1, 2 sc into next sc * five times.
Rnd 3: * Sc 2, 2 sc into next sc * five times.
Rnd 4: * Sc 3, 2 sc into next sc * five times.
Rnd 5: * Sc 4, 2 sc into next sc * five times.
Rnds 6–12: Sc 1 all around.
Rnd 13: * Sc 4, skip 1, 1 sc * five times.
Rnd 14: Sc 1 all around.
Rnd 15: * Sc 3, skip 1, 1 sc * five times.
Rnd 16: Sc 1 all around.
Rnd 17: * Sc 2, skip 1 * five times.
Rnds 18–21: Sc 1 all around.
Fasten off, leaving a long tail end.

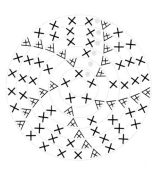

Body

NOSE

Make a loop as you did for the body, and 5 sc into the circle.

Rnd 1: Sc 2 into each of 5 sc.

Rnd 2: * Sc 1, 2 sc into next sc * five times.

Rnd 3: * Sc 2, 2 sc into next sc * five times. Fasten off.

Nose

EARS (MAKE TWO)

Ch 7, fasten off.

TAIL

Use the long ends left over when you fastened off the body to make the tail. Twist the yarn end until it doubles up on itself and makes a tiny spiral tail.

MATERIALS

E-4 (3.5 mm) hook
Angora in cream (for head and body)
Red wool scrap (body)
Light pink yarn scrap (nose)
Plastic eyes ¼ in. (7 mm) diameter
Red embroidery floss (for mouth)
Red felt (for cheeks) and white felt (for tiny teeth)

MEASUREMENTS

6 in. (15 cm) tall

DIRECTIONS

HEAD

Make a loop with tail end of yarn on right, keeping ball end on left. Pull the ball end of yarn through loop. Make one chain through loop on hook you have drawn through to steady the circle.

Work 5 sc in to the circle and complete the circle with Sl st in to the first sc.

Rnd 1: Sc 2 into each of 5 sc.
Rnd 2: * Sc 1, 2 sc into next sc * five times.
Rnd 3: * Sc 2, 2 sc into next sc * five times.
Rnds 4–7: Sc 1 into each sc.
Rnd 8: * Sc 2, skip 1 * five times.
Rnd 9: * Sc 1, skip 1 * five times.
Rnd 10: * Sc 1, skip 1 * repeat all around.
Fasten off.

BODY

Using red wool first, make a loop as you did for the body, and sc 5 into the circle.

Rnd 1: Sc 2 into each of 5 sc.
Rnd 2: * Sc 1, 2 sc into next sc, * five times.
Rnd 3: * Sc 2, 2 sc into next sc * five times.
Rnd 4: * Sc 3, 2 sc into next sc * five times.
Rnds 5–7: Sc 1 all around (change the color to cream).
Rnds 8–9: Sc 1 all around in cream, then change the color to red.
Rnds 10–11: Sc 1 into each sc in red.
Rnds 12–13: Sc 1 into each sc in cream.
Rnds 14–15: Sc 1 all around in red then change the color to cream.
Add stuffing at this point.
Rnd 16: * Sc 3, skip 1 * five times.
Rnd 17: * Sc 2, skip 1 * five times.
Rnd 18: * Sc 1, skip 1 * repeat all around.
Fasten off.

10
9
8
4 - 7

Head

18
17
16
5 - 15

Body

MUZZLE

Using cream, make a loop as before and sc 5 into the circle.

Rnd 1: Sc 2 into each st.
Rnd 2: * Sc 1, 2 sc into next sc, * five times.
Rnd 3: * Sc 2, 2 sc into next sc, * five times.
Fasten off.

EARS (MAKE TWO)

Make 5 chains.

Rows 1–5: Ch 1, 1 sc to end.
Row 6: Sc2tog, 1 sc to last 2 st, sc2tog.
Row 7: Ch 1, 1 sc to end.
Sc 1 all around edge; fasten off.

NOSE

Using light pink yarn, make a loop as before and sc 3 into the circle.

Rnd 1: Sc 2 into each st.
Rnd 2: * Sc 1, 2 sc into next sc, * three times.
Rnd 3: Sc 1 all around.
Fasten off.

ARMS (MAKE TWO)

Using cream colored yarn, make a loop as before and sc 5 into the circle to start.

Rnd 1: 2 sc into each st.
Rnd 2: * Sc 1, 2 sc into next sc * five times.
Rnd 3: * Sc 2, 2 sc into next sc * five times.
Rnds 4–7: Sc 1 all around.
Rnd 8: * Sc 2, skip 1 * five times, sc 1.
Rnd 9: Sc 1 all around.
Rnd 10: Sc 1, skip 1 * five times, sc 1.
Rnds 11–12: Sc 1 all around and fasten off.
No need to stuff, make them look flappy.

LEGS (MAKE TWO)

Make these in the same way as the arms but sc 1 all around from rnds 4–10 before decreasing.

Muzzle

Arms

Ears

Nose

Rabbit's ears
Fold the ears at the base, when
you sew them to the head, to
create a three-dimensional ear.

Body
Dark colors near the base
will balance visually.

Smile
please!

Penguins

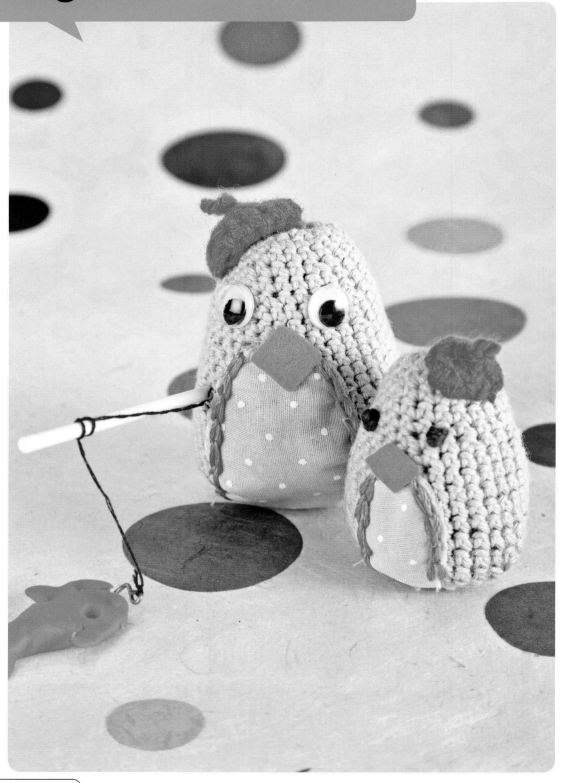

MATERIALS

C-2 (2.75 mm) hook
Pale blue cotton
Plastic eyes ¼ in. (7 mm) diameter
Scrap of red yarn (for hat)
Scrap fabric (for a bib)
Orange felt (for beak)

MEASUREMENTS

2 ¾in. (7 cm) tallest

DIRECTIONS

BODY

Make a loop with tail end of yarn on right, keeping ball end on left. Pull the ball end through loop. Make one chain through loop on hook you have drawn through to steady the circle. Sc 5 into the circle and complete with Sl st in to the first sc.

Rnd 1: Sc 2 into each of 5 sc.
Rnd 2: * Sc 1, 2 sc into next sc * five times.
Rnd 3: * Sc 2, 2 sc into next sc * five times.
Rnd 4: * Sc 3, 2 sc into next sc * five times.
Rnd 5: * Sc 4, 2 sc into next sc * five times.

Rnds 6–10: Sc 1 all around.
Rnd 11: * Sc 4, skip 1 * five times.
Rnd 12: Sc 1 all around.
Rnd 13: * Sc 3, skip 1 * five times.
Rnds 14–15: Sc 1 all around.
Rnd 16: * Sc 2, skip 1 * five times.
Rnds 17–19: Sc 1 all around.
Rnd 20: *Sc 1, skip 1 * five times.
Rnd 21: Sc 1 all around.
Rnd 22: *Sc 1, skip 1 * five times.
Fasten off.

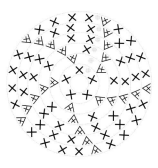

Body

TINY HAT

Make a loop as you did for the body, and 5 sc into the circle.

Rnd 1: Sc 2 into each of 5 sc.

Rnd 2: * Sc 1, 2 sc in to next sc * five times.

Rnds 3–4: Sc 1 all around.

Fasten off. Leave a long end, to make a small bobble on top of the hat.

××××××××××××××× 3-4

Tiny hat

Teeny tiny hat

BABY PENGUIN

BODY

Make a loop with tail end of yarn on right, keeping ball end on left. Pull the ball end through loop. Make one chain through loop on hook you have drawn through to steady the circle. Sc 5 into the circle and complete with Sl st in to the first sc.

Rnd 1: 2 sc into each 5 sc.

Rnd 2: * Sc 1, 2 sc into next sc * five times.

Rnd 3: * Sc 2, 2 sc into next sc * five times.

Rnd 4: * Sc 3, 2 sc into next sc * five times.

Rnds 5–10: Sc 1 all around.

Rnd 11: * Sc 3, skip 1, * five times.

Rnd 12: Sc 1 all around.

Rnd 13: * Sc 2, skip 1, * five times.

Rnds 14–15: Sc 1 all around.

Rnds 16–17: * Sc 1, skip 1, * five times.

Fasten off.

TEENY TINY HAT

Make a loop as you did for the body, and 5 sc into the circle.

Rnd 1: Sc 2 into each 5 sc.

Rnd 2–3: Sc 1 all around.

Fasten off. Leave a long end, to make a small bobble on top of the hat.

16–17
14–15
13
12
11
5–10

Baby body

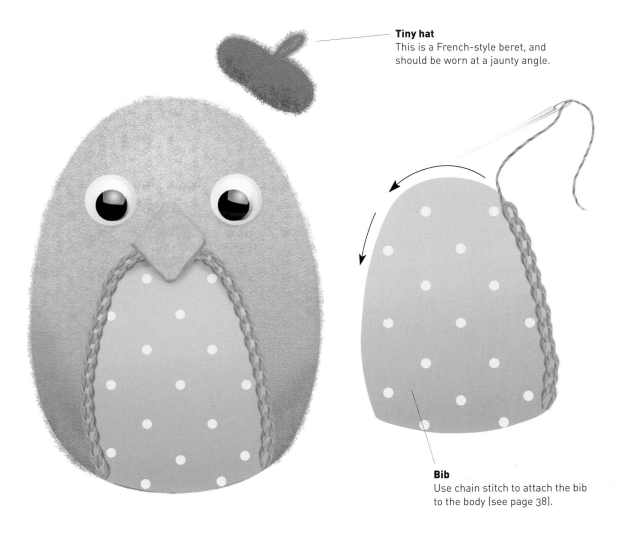

Tiny hat
This is a French-style beret, and should be worn at a jaunty angle.

Bib
Use chain stitch to attach the bib to the body (see page 38).

Penguins

Bear

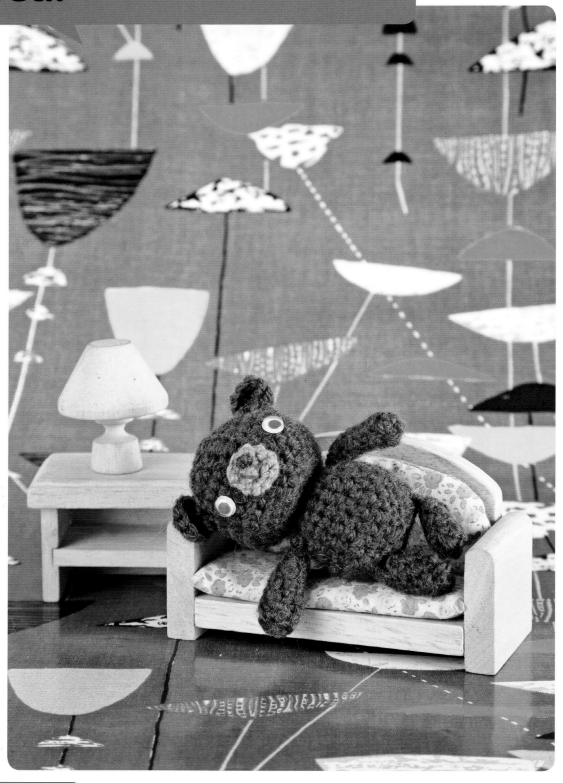

MATERIALS

E-4 (3.5 mm) hook
Brown yarn
Light brown yarn (for muzzle)
Red embroidery floss (for mouth)
Plastic eyes ¼ in. (7 mm) diameter

MEASUREMENTS

3½ in. (9 cm) tall

DIRECTIONS

BODY

Make a loop with tail end of yarn on right, keeping ball end on left. Pull the ball end through loop. Make one chain through loop on hook you have drawn through to steady the circle. Sc 5 into the circle and complete with Sl st in to the first sc.

Rnd 1: Sc 2 into each of 5 sc.
Rnd 2: * Sc 1, 2 sc into next sc * five times.
Rnd 3: * Sc 2, 2 sc into next sc * five times.
Rnd 4: * Sc 3, 2 sc into next sc * five times.
Rnds 5–7: Sc all around.
Rnd 8: * Sc 3, skip 1, 1 sc * five times.
Rnd 9: * Sc 2, skip 1, 1 sc * five times.
          Add stuffing at this point.
Rnd 10: * Sc 1, skip 1, 1 sc * five times.
Rnd 11: * Sc 1, skip 1 * five times.
Fasten off.

HEAD

Make a loop as before and 5 sc into the circle to start.

Rnd 1: Sc 2 into each of the 5 sc.
Rnd 2: * Sc 1, 2 sc into next sc * five times.
Rnd 3: * Sc 2, 2 sc into next sc * five times.
Rnd 4: * Sc 3, 2 sc into next sc * five times.
Rnds 5–9: Sc all around.
Rnd 10: * Sc 3, skip 1, 1 sc * five times.
Rnd 11: * Sc 2, skip 1, 1 sc * five times.
          Add stuffing at this point.
Rnd 12: * Sc 1, skip 1, 1 sc * five times.
Rnd 13: * Sc 1, skip 1 * five times.
Fasten off.

11
10
9
8
5 - 7

13
12
11
10
5 - 9

Body

Head

EARS [MAKE TWO]

Make a loop as before and 5 sc into the circle to start.
Rnd 1: Sc 2 into each of 5 sc.
Rnd 2: * Sc 1, 2 sc into next sc * five times.
Fasten off.

MUZZLE

With light brown yarn, make a loop as before and sc 5 into the circle to start.
Rnd 1: Sc 2 into each of 5 sc.
Rnd 2: * Sc 1, 2 sc into next sc * five times.
Fasten off.

ARMS [MAKE TWO]

Make a loop as before and sc 5 into the circle to start.
Rnd 1: Sc 2 into each st.
Rnds 2–6: Sc 1 all around.
Rnd 7: * Sc 1, skip 1 * five times.
Fasten off.
No need to stuff them.

LEGS [MAKE TWO]

Make a loop as before and sc 5 into the circle to start.
Rnd 1: Sc 2 into each st.
Rnds 2–4: Sc 1 all around.
Rnd 5: * Sc 1, skip 1 * five times.
Fasten off.
No need to stuff them.

Ears/muzzle

Arms/legs

Legs
For the legs, follow the arm chart but go straight from rows 2–4.

My jokes are unbearable

Features
Sew the muzzle onto the face and decorate with a French-knot nose and a red mouth.

Baby bear

Cocktail time!

Grumpy tiny mohair bear

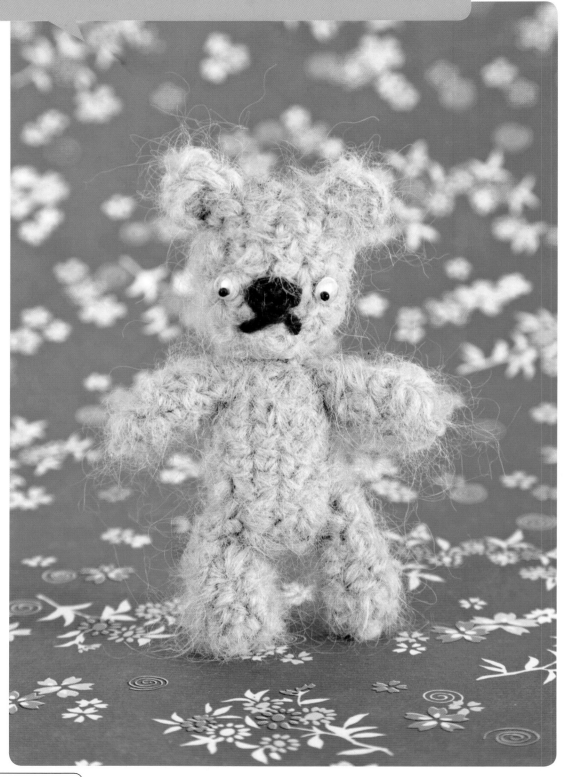

MATERIALS

C-2 (2.75 mm) hook
Brown mohair
Dark brown yarn (for nose and mouth)
Plastic eyes 1³⁄₁₆ in. (3 mm) diameter

MEASUREMENTS

2¾ in. (7 cm) tall

DIRECTIONS

BODY

Make a loop with tail end of yarn on right, keeping ball
end on left. Pull the ball end through loop.
Make one chain through loop on hook you have drawn
through to steady the circle.
Work 5 sc in to the circle and complete the circle with
Sl st into the first sc.
Rnd 1: Sc 2 into each 5 sc.
Rnd 2: * Sc 1, 2 sc into next sc * five times.
Rnds 3–7: Sc 1 all around.
Rnd 8: * Sc 1, skip 1, 1 sc * five times.
          Add stuffing at this point.
Rnd 9: Sc 1 all around.
Rnd 10: * Sc 1, skip 1 * five times.
Fasten off.

HEAD

Make a loop as before and 5 sc into the circle to start.
Rnd 1: Sc 2 into each 5 sc.
Rnd 2: * Sc 1, 2 sc into next sc * five times.
Rnd 3: * Sc 2, 2 sc into next sc * five times.
Rnds 4–5: Sc 1 all around.
Rnd 6: * Sc 2, skip 1, 1 sc * five times.
          Add stuffing at this point.
Rnd 7: * Sc 1, skip 1, 1 sc * five times.
Rnd 8: * Sc 1, skip 1 * five times.
Fasten off.

Body

Head

EARS [MAKE TWO]

Make a loop as before and sc 3 into the circle to start.

Rnd 1: 2 sc into each 3 sc.

Fasten off.

Ears

ARMS AND LEGS [MAKE FOUR]

Make a loop as before and 3 sc into the circle to start.

Rnd 1: 2 sc into each st.

Rnds 2–6: Sc 1 all around.

Rnd 7: * Sc 1, skip 1 * three times.

Fasten off; no need to stuff.

Arms/legs

I can't bear it anymore

Features
Make a nose in dark brown yarn by making 3 ch and attaching. Make a suitably down-turned mouth.

Grumpy tiny mohair bear

Tanuki

MATERIALS

E-4 (3.5 mm) hook
Dark orange and light orange acrylic yarn
Plastic eyes ⅜ in. (10 mm) diameter
Brown embroidery floss (for belly button)

MEASUREMENTS

4½ in. (11 cm) tall

DIRECTIONS

BODY

Using dark orange first: make a loop with tail end of yarn on right, keeping ball end on left. Pull the ball end through loop. Make one chain through loop on hook you have drawn through to steady the circle. Work 5 sc into the circle and complete with Sl st in to the first sc.

Rnd 1: Sc 2 into each 5 sc.

Rnd 2: * Sc 1, 2 sc into next sc * five times.

Rnd 3: * Sc 2, 2 sc into next sc * five times.

Rnd 4: * Sc 3, 2 sc into next sc * five times.

Rnd 5: * Sc 4, 2 sc into next sc * five times.

Rnds 6–7: Sc 1 into each st. Change to light orange.

Rnds 8–9: Sc 1 into each st, then change to dark orange.

Rnd 10: * Sc 4, skip 1, 1 sc * five times.

Rnd 11: * Sc 3, skip 1, 1 sc * five times. Change color to light orange.

Rnd 12: * Sc 2, skip 1, 1 sc * five times. Add stuffing at this point.

Rnd 13: * Sc 1, skip 1, 1 sc * five times.

Rnd 14: * Sc 1, skip 1 * five times.

Fasten off.

FACE

Using dark orange first, make a loop as you did for the body, and sc 5 into the circle.

Rnd 1: Sc 2 into each of 5 sc.

Rnd 2: * Sc 1, 2 sc into next sc * five times.

Rnd 3: * Sc 2, 2 sc into next sc * five times.

Rnd 4: * Sc 3, 2 sc * five times.

Rnds 5–9: Sc 1 all around.

Rnd 10: * Sc 3, skip 1 * five times.

Rnd 11: Change the color to light orange for the face.
* Sc 2, skip 1, 1 sc, * five times.
Add stuffing at this point.

Rnd 12: * Sc 1, skip 1, 1 sc * five times.

Rnd 13: Sc 1 all around.

Rnd 14: * Sc 1, skip 1 * five times.

Fasten off.

Body

Face

TAIL

Using dark orange yarn first, make a loop as before and 5 sc into the circle.

Rnd 1: Sc 2 into each st.
Rnd 2: * Sc 1, 2 sc into next st * five times.
Rnd 3: * Sc 2, 2 sc into next st * five times.
Rnd 4: * Sc 3, 2 sc into next st,* five times.
Rnds 5–8: Sc 1 into each st then change the color to light orange.
Rnds 9–11: Sc 1 into each st then change the color to dark orange.
Rnd 12: * Sc 3, skip 1, 1 sc * five times.
Rnd 13: Sc 1 all around, then change the color to light orange.
Rnd 14: as rnd 13.
Rnd 15: * Sc 2, skip 1, 1sc * five times, then change the color to dark orange.
Rnds 16–20: Sc 1 all around.
Fasten off.

Tail

EARS (MAKE TWO)

Using light orange first, make a loop as before and 5 sc into the circle to start.

Rnd 1: Sc 2 into each st.
Rnd 2: * Sc 1, 2 sc into next stitch, * five times, then change the color to dark orange.
Rnd 3: * Sc 2, 2 sc into next stitch, * five times.
Fasten off.

EYES (MAKE TWO)

Using dark orange yarn, make a loop as before and 5 sc into the circle to start.

Rnd 1: Sc 2 into each st.
Rnd 2: * Sc 1, 2 sc into next st, * five times.
Rnd 3: * Sc 2, 2 sc into next st, * five times.
Fasten off.

Eyes/ears

ARMS (MAKE TWO)

Using dark orange yarn, make a loop as before and 5 sc into the circle to start.

Rnd 1: Sc 2 into each st.
Rnd 2: * Sc 1, 2 sc into next st, * five times.
Rnd 3: * Sc 2, 2 sc into next st, * five times.
Rnds 4–7: Sc 1 all around.
Rnd 8: * Sc 2, skip 1 * five times.
Rnd 9: Sc 1 all around.
Rnd 10: Sc 1, skip 1 * five times.
Rnds 11–12: Sc 1 all around.
Fasten off; no need to stuff.

Arms

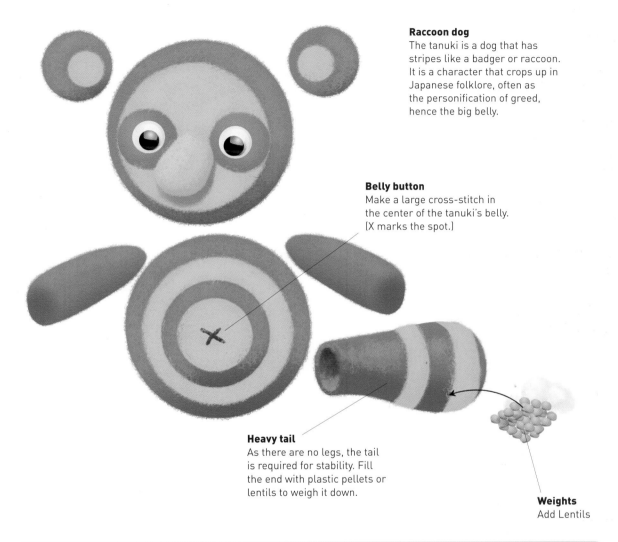

Raccoon dog
The tanuki is a dog that has stripes like a badger or raccoon. It is a character that crops up in Japanese folklore, often as the personification of greed, hence the big belly.

Belly button
Make a large cross-stitch in the center of the tanuki's belly. (X marks the spot.)

Heavy tail
As there are no legs, the tail is required for stability. Fill the end with plastic pellets or lentils to weigh it down.

Weights
Add Lentils

Tanuki raccoon dog

MATERIALS

E-4 (3.5 mm) hook
Rust-brown yarn (for body)
Orange and yellow yarn (for mane and tail)
Orange felt (for nose and feet)
Plastic eyes ⅜ in. (10 mm) diameter
Brown embroidery floss

MEASUREMENTS

4 in. (10 cm) tall

DIRECTIONS

BODY

Make a loop with tail end of yarn on right, keeping ball
end on left. Pull the ball end through loop. Make one
chain through loop on hook you have drawn through to
steady the circle.
Work 5 sc into the circle and complete the circle with
Sl st into the first sc.
Rnd 1: Sc 2 into each 5 sc.
Rnd 2: * Sc 1, 2 sc into next sc * five times.
Rnd 3: * Sc 2, 2 sc into next sc * five times.
Rnd 4: * Sc 3, 2 sc into next sc * five times.
Rnd 5: * Sc 4, 2 sc into next sc * five times.
Rnds 6–10: Sc 1 all around.
Rnd 11: * Sc 4, skip 1, 1 sc * five times.
Rnds 12–13: Sc 1 all around.
Rnd 14: * Sc 3, skip 1, 1 sc * five times.
Rnds 15–16: Sc 1 all around.
Rnd 17: * Sc 2, skip 1, 1 sc * five times.
Rnd 18: * Sc 1, skip 1, 1 sc * five times.
Rnd 19: * Sc 1, skip 1 * five times.
Fasten off.

MANE (MAKE TWO)

Ch 36.
Row 1: * Ch 1, 5 sc into the first st, skip 1, 1 sc
in next st. Repeat from * to end.
Make one with orange and one with yellow.

TAIL

Make a tiny tassel with orange yarn then attach to
18 chains in brown.

Body

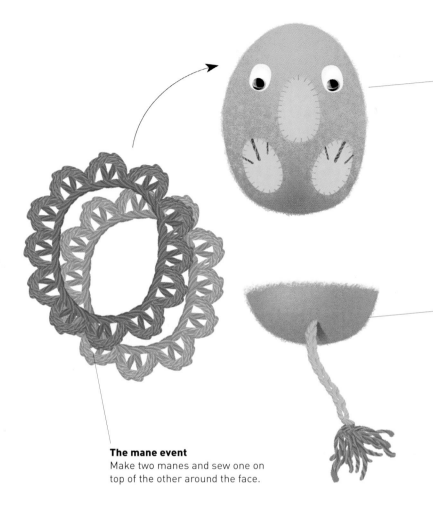

Features
Nose and feet are made from orange felt. Make feet with large stitches in brown embroidery floss.

Tail
Make 18 ch and attach to back with an orange tassel on the end.

The mane event
Make two manes and sew one on top of the other around the face.

Fierce lion

Magpies

MATERIALS

C-2 (2.75 mm) hook
Black yarn
Scrap of white yarn (for tummy)
Orange felt (for beak)
Plastic eyes ⅜ in. x 3⁄16 in. (10 mm x 5 mm)

MEASUREMENTS

2½ in. (6.5 cm) tall

DIRECTIONS

BODY AND HEAD

Make a loop with tail end of yarn on right, keeping ball end on left. Pull the ball end through loop. Make one chain through loop on hook you have drawn through to steady the circle.

Work 5 sc in to the circle and complete the circle with Sl st in to the first sc.

Rnd 1: Sc 2 into each of 5 sc.
Rnd 2: * Sc 1, 2 sc into next sc * five times.
Rnd 3: * Sc 2, 2 sc into next sc * five times.
Rnd 4: * Sc 3, 2 sc * five times.
Rnds 5–9: Sc 1 all around.
Rnd 10: * Sc 3, skip 1 * five times.
Rnd 11: * Sc 2, skip 1 * five times.
     Add stuffing at this point.
Rnd 12–14: Sc 1 all around.
Rnd 15: * Sc 1, skip 1 * five times.
Rnd 16: * Sc 1, skip 1 * five times.
Fasten off.

Body

TAIL

Ch 12, then join the first chain and the last one with sl st.

Rnds 1–2: Sc 1 all around.

Rnd 3: * Sc 1, skip 1, repeat from * all around.

Rnd 4: Sc 1 all around.

Rnd 5: * Sc 1, skip 1, repeat from * all around until 4 sts are left.

Fasten off.

WINGS (MAKE TWO)

Ch 8.

Row 1: Ch 1, sc 1 into each of the first 2 sts, 1 dc, 1 tr in each next 2 sts, 1 dc, 1 sc to end.

Fasten off.

Wings

Features
These plastic eyes are extra large
for the size of the face.

Belly
Use satin stitch
to make the white
front as shown.

Tail
Sew the fat end of the tail
to the back, so that it helps
with balance. Stuff with
pellets or tufts of yarn.

Magpie

Sausage dog

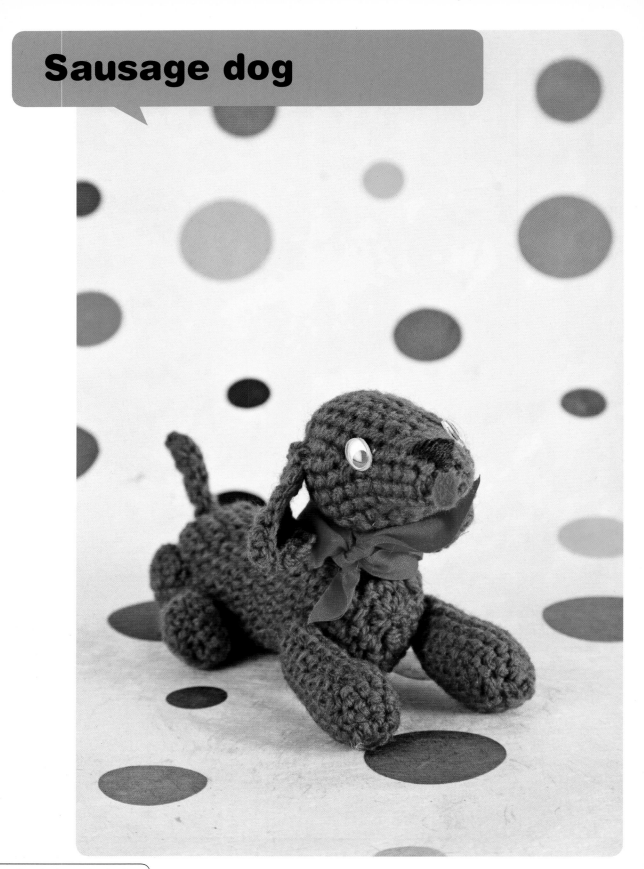

MATERIALS

E-4 (3.5 mm) hook
Brown yarn
Plastic eyes ⅜ in. x ³⁄₁₆ in. (10 mm x 5 mm)
Dark brown embroidery floss (for nose)
Red felt (for tongue)

MEASUREMENTS

6 ⅜ in. (16 cm) tall

DIRECTIONS

BODY

Make a loop with tail end of yarn on right, keeping ball end on left. Pull the ball end through loop. Make one chain through loop on hook you have drawn through to steady the circle. Work 5 sc in to the circle and complete the circle with Sl st in to the first sc.

Rnd 1: Sc 2 into each of 5 sc.
Rnd 2: * Sc 1, 2 sc into next sc * five times.
Rnd 3: * Sc 2, 2 sc into next sc * five times.
Rnds 4–18: Sc 1 all around.
Rnd 19: * Sc 2, skip 1, 1 sc * five times.
　　　　　Add stuffing at this point.
Rnd 20: * Sc 1, skip 1, 1 sc * five times.
Rnd 21: * Sc 1, skip 1 * five times.
Fasten off.

NECK

Using brown yarn, ch 15, join the first chain and last one with Sl st to form the circle.
Rnds 1–5: Sc 1 into each st.
Fasten off.

HEAD

Using brown yarn, make a loop as you did for the body, and 5 sc into the circle.
Rnd 1: Sc 2 into each of 5 sc.
Rnd 2: * Sc 1, 2 sc into next sc * five times.
Rnd 3: * Sc 2, 2 sc into next sc * five times.
Rnd 4: * Sc 3, 2 sc into next sc * five times.
Rnds 5–9: Sc 1 all around.
Rnd 10: * Sc 3, skip 1, 1 sc * five times.
Rnd 11: Sc 1 all around.
Rnd 12: * Sc 2, skip 1, 1 sc * five times.
Rnds 13–14: Sc 1 all around.
Rnd 15: * Sc 1, skip 1, 1 sc * five times.
Rnds 16–18: Sc 1 all around.
Rnd 19: * Sc 1, skip 1 * repeat all around.
Fasten off.

Body

Head

FRONT LEGS (MAKE TWO)

Make a loop as before and 5 sc into the circle to start.

Rnd 1: Sc 2 into each st.
Rnd 2: * Sc 1, 2 sc into each st * five times.
Rnd 3: * Sc 2, 2 sc into each st * five times.
Rnds 4–6: Sc 1 all around.
Rnd 7: * Sc 2, skip 1, 1 sc * five times.
Rnd 8: Sc 1 all around.
Rnd 9: * Sc 1, skip 1, 1 sc * five times.
Rnd 10: * Sc 1, skip 1 * five times.
Fasten off.

Front legs

EARS (MAKE TWO)

Ch 6 to start.

Row 1: 1 ch, then 1 sc into each st to the end. Turn.
Row 2: 1 ch, then 1 sc into each st to the end. Turn.
Row 3: Sc 1 into next each 5 sts. Turn.
Rows 4–5: Ch 1, 1 sc to end. Turn.
Row 6: Sc 1 into next 4 sts. Turn.
Row 7: Ch 1, 1 sc to end.
Sc 1 all around the edge and fasten off.

TAIL (FOLD INTO HALF)

Ch 4.

Rows 1–4: Ch 1, 1 sc to end, turn.
Row 5: Sc 1 into next 3 sts.
Rows 6–8: Ch 1, 1 sc to end.
Fasten off.

Ears

Tail

BACK LEGS (MAKE TWO)

SECTION 1

Make a loop as before and 5 sc into the circle to start.

Rnd 1: Sc 2 into each st.
Rnd 2: * Sc 1, 2 sc into next st * five times.
Rnds 3–5: Sc 1 all around.
Rnd 6: *Sc 1, skip 1 * five times.
Rnds 7–9: Sc 1 all around.
Fasten off.

Section 1

SECTION 2

Make a loop as before and 5 sc into the circle to start.

Rnd 1: Sc 2 into each st.
Rnd 2: * Sc 1, 2 sc into next st * five times.
Rnd 3: * Sc 2, 2 sc into next st * five times.
Rnds 4–6: Sc 1 all around, and fasten off.

Section 2

Tongue
Attach red felt
tongue so it is
hanging out.

Ears
Position the ears low
down on the head, so that
they are long and floppy.

Neck section
Attach the small ring that
forms the neck to the end
of the body, and fill with
a little stuffing to keep
his head held high.

Tail
Fold the tail section in half
along its length, and sew up,
then sew on so that it stands
up proudly.

Sausage dog

Owl

MATERIALS

E-4 (3.5 mm) hook
Brown yarn
Purple fine mohair (for embellishments)
White yarn (for eyes)
Plastic eyes ¼ in. (7 mm) diameter
Orange felt (for beak)

MEASUREMENTS

2¾ in. (7 cm) tall

DIRECTIONS

BODY

Make a loop with tail end of yarn on right, keeping ball end on left. Pull the ball end of yarn through loop. Make one chain through loop on hook you have drawn through to steady the circle.

Work 5 sc in to the circle and complete the circle with Sl st in to the first sc.

Rnd 1: Sc 2 into each of 5 sc.
Rnd 2: * Sc 1, 2 sc into next sc * five times.
Rnd 3: * Sc 2, 2 sc into next sc * five times.
Rnd 4: * Sc 3, 2 sc into next sc * five times.
Rnds 5–18: Sc 1 all around.
Fasten off.

BOTTOM

Make a circle as before, work 5 sc in to the circle and complete the circle with a Sl st in to the first sc.
Rnd 1: Sc 2 into each of 5 sc.
Rnd 2: * Sc 1, 2 sc into next sc * five times.
Rnd 3: * Sc 2, 2 sc into next sc * five times.
Rnd 4: * Sc 3, 2 sc into next sc * five times.
Fasten off.

×××××××××××××××××××××××× 5–18

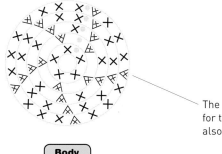

The circle chart for the body is also the base.

Body

TUMMY

Using purple mohair, ch 14.

Row 1: Sc 1 into 6th ch from hook. * Ch 5, skip 3, 1 sc into next ch: rep from * to end then turn.

Row 2: * 5 ch, 1 sc into next 5 ch arch. Repeat from * to end then turn.

Repeat these 2 rows.

WINGS (MAKE TWO)

Ch 5.

Row 1: Sc 1 to end.

Row 2: Ch 1, 1 sc to last 2 st, sc2tog.

Row 3: Ch 1, 1 sc to end.

Fasten off.

Wings

EYES (MAKE TWO)

Make a loop as you did for the body, and 5 sc into the circle.

Rnd 1: Sc 2 into each of 5 sc.

Rnd 2: * Sc 1, 2 sc in to next sc * five times, then change the color to purple.

Rnd 3: * Sc 2, 2 sc * five times.

Fasten off.

Eyes

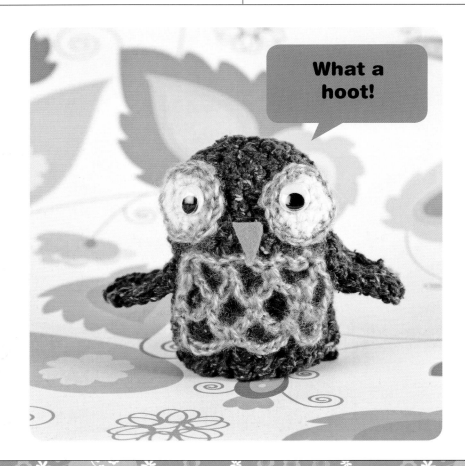

What a hoot!

Features
Sew on the eye patches, and glue on plastic eyes. Sew on the belly pattern. Make a small beak out of orange felt.

Wings
Attach the wings on either side, so that they point backward, like this.

Stuffing
Complete all the features before finishing. Insert stuffing from the base end, then sew base in place.

Owl

Monkey

MATERIALS

E-4 (3.5 mm) hook
Brown yarn (for body)
Light brown yarn (for face)
Plastic eyes ⅜ in. x 3/16 in. (10 mm x 5 mm)
Red embroidery floss (for mouth)
Brown embroidery floss (for nose)

MEASUREMENTS

6⅜ in. (16 cm) tall

GAUGE

12 st x 10 rows = 2 in. (5 cm)

DIRECTIONS

BODY

Make a loop with tail end of yarn on right, keeping ball end on left. Pull the ball end through loop. Make one chain through loop on hook you have drawn through to steady the circle. Work 5 sc in to the circle and complete the circle with Sl st in to the first sc.

Rnd 1: Sc 2 into each 5 sc.
Rnd 2: * Sc 1, 2 sc into next sc * five times.
Rnd 3: * Sc 2, 2 sc into next sc * five times.
Rnds 4–11: Sc 1 into each sc.
Rnd 12: * Sc 2, skip 1, 1 sc * five times.
Rnds 13–14: Sc 1 all around.
　　　　Add stuffing at this point.
Rnd 15: * Sc 1, skip 1, 1 sc * five times.
Rnds 16–18: Sc 1 all around.
Rnd 19: Sc 1 into every other st.
Fasten off.

FACE

Make a loop as you did for the body, and 5 sc into the circle.

Rnd 1: Sc 2 into each 5 sc.
Rnd 2: * Sc 1, 2 sc in to next sc * five times.
Rnd 3: * Sc 2, 2 sc in to next sc * five times.
Rnd 4: * Sc 3, 2 sc in to next sc * five times.
Rnds 5–9: Sc 1 all around.
Rnd 10: * Sc 3, skip 1, 1 sc * five times.
　　　　Change the color to light brown for the face.
Rnd 11: * Sc 2, skip 1, 1 sc * five times.
　　　　Add stuffing at this point.
Rnd 12: * Sc 1, skip 1, 1 sc * five times.
Rnd 13: * Sc 1, skip 1 * five times.
Fasten off.

19
16 - 18
15
13, 14
12
4 - 11

Body

13
12
11
10
5 - 9

Face

MUZZLE

Using light brown yarn, make a loop as before and 5 sc into the circle.

Rnd 1: Sc 2 into each st.
Rnd 2: * Sc 1, 2 sc into next st * five times.
Rnd 3: * Sc 1, 1 sc, into next st * five times.
Rnds 4–6: Sc 1 around.
Rnd 7–8: * Sc 1, skip 1 * all around.
Fasten off.

EARS (MAKE TWO)

Make a loop as before and 5 sc into the circle to start.
Start with the light brown yarn
Rnd 1: Sc 2 into each of 5 sc , then change the color to brown yarn.
Rnd 2: * Sc 1, 2 sc into next sc * five times.
Fasten off.

ARMS (MAKE TWO)

Using brown yarn, make a loop as before, and sc 5 into the circle to start.

Rnd 1: Sc 2 into each st.
Rnd 2: * Sc 1, 2 sc into next st * five times.
Rnd 3: * Sc 2, 2 sc into next st * five times.
Rnds 4–10: Sc 1 all around.
Rnd 11: * Sc 2, skip 1 * five times.
Rnd 12: * Sc 1, skip 1 * five times.
　　　　　Add stuffing at this point.
Rnd 13: * Sc 1, skip 1 * five times.
Fasten off.

LEGS (MAKE TWO)

Make these in the same way as making the arms, but sc 1 all around from rnd 4–7 before decreasing.

Arms/legs

Ears

4 - 6

Muzzle

Features
Attach the muzzle with
a little stuffing to make
it stand out. Make a big
smile with red yarn and
chain stitch.

**Monkey see,
monkey do**

Panda bear

MATERIALS

E-4 (3.5 mm) hook
Black and white acrylic yarns
Plastic eyes 3/8 in. x 3/16 in. (10 mm x 5 mm)
Red embroidery floss (for mouth)

MEASUREMENTS

6 3/8 in. (16 cm) tall

DIRECTIONS

BODY

Using black yarn, make a loop as before and 5 sc into the circle.

Rnd 1: Sc 2 into each of 5 sc.
Rnd 2: * Sc 1, 2 sc into next sc * five times.
Rnd 3: * Sc 2, 2 sc into next sc * five times.
Rnd 4: * Sc 3, 2 sc into next sc * five times.
Rnds 5–7: Sc 1 around (change the color to white).
Rnds 8–9: Sc 1 around in white, then change to black.
Rnds 10–11: Sc 1 around in black.
Rnds 12–13 : Sc 1 around in white.
Rnds14–15: Sc 1 around in white, then change the color to black yarn. Add stuffing at this point.
Rnd 16: * Sc 3, skip 1, 1 sc * five times.
Rnd 17: * Sc 2, skip 1 * five times, 1 sc.
Rnd 18: * Sc 1, skip 1 * all around.
Fasten off.

HEAD

Make a loop with tail end of yarn on right, keeping ball end on left. Pull the ball end through loop. Make one chain through loop on hook you have drawn through to steady the circle. Work 5 sc in to the circle and complete the circle with Sl st in to the first sc.

Rnd 1: Sc 2 into each of 5 sc.
Rnd 2: * Sc 1, 2 sc into next sc * five times.
Rnd 3: * Sc 2, 2 sc into next sc * five times.
Rnds 4–7: Sc 1 all around.
Rnd 8: * Sc 2, skip 1 * five times.
Rnd 9: * Sc 1, skip 1 * five times.
Rnd 10: Sc 1 into every alternate st.
Fasten off.

Body

Head

NOSE

Using black yarn, make a loop as before and 5 sc into the circle.

Rnd 1: Sc 2 into each st.
Rnd 2: * Sc 1, 2 sc into next sc * five times.
Rnd 3: * Sc 2, 2 sc into next sc * five times.
Rnd 4: * Sc 2, skip 1 * five times.
Fasten off.

EYES (MAKE 2)

Using black yarn, make a loop as before and 3 sc into the circle.

Rnd 1: 2 sc into each st.
Rnd 2: * Sc 1, 2 sc into each st * three times.
Rnd 3: Sc 1 into next 4 st.
Row 4: Turn without making ch, 1 sc into next 3 sc.
Row 5: Turn with 1 ch, 1 sc into next 3 sc.
Fasten off.

EARS (MAKE 2)

Using black yarn, make a loop as before and 3 sc into the circle.

Rnd 1: Sc 2 into each st.
Rnd 2: * Sc 1, 2 sc into next st * three times.
Rnd 3: * Sc 2, 2 sc into next st * three times.
Rnd 4: * Sc 3, 2 sc into next st * three times.
Fasten off.

ARMS AND LEGS (MAKE 4)

Using black, make a loop as before and 5 sc into the circle to start.

Rnd 1: Sc 2 into each st.
Rnd 2: * Sc 1, 2 sc into next st * five times.
Rnd 3: * Sc 2, 2 sc into next st * five times.
Rnds 4–10: Sc 1 all around.
Rnd 11: * Sc 2, skip 1 * five times.
Add stuffing at this point.
Rnd 12: Sc 1, skip 1 * five times.
Rnd 13: * Sc 1, skip 1 * five times.
Fasten off.

Nose

Eyes

Ears

Arms

Features
Sew on nose and eye patches.
Glue on plastic eyes and make
a chain-stitch mouth in red yarn.

Superhero
Panda

Field mouse

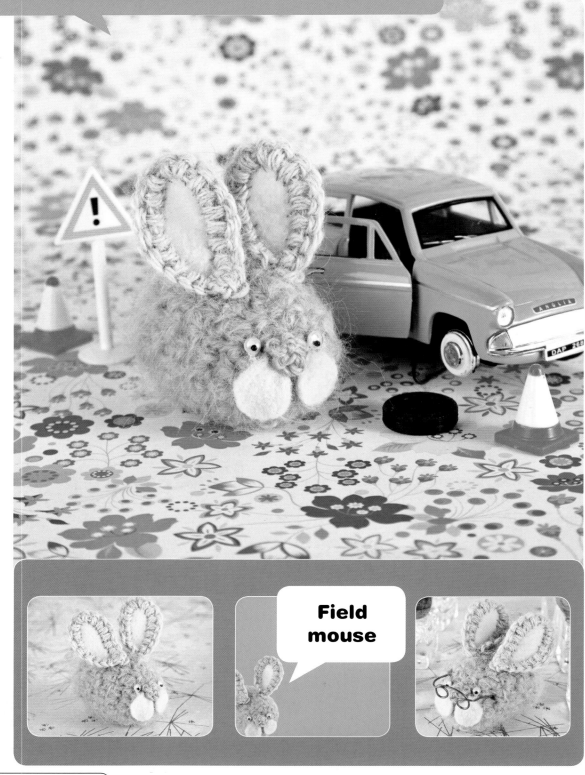

Field mouse

MATERIALS

C-2 (2.75 mm) hook
White mohair
Scrap of pink yarn (for nose)
Plastic eyes ⅛ in. (3 mm) diameter
Cream felt (for ears and cheeks)

MEASUREMENTS

2¼ in. (6 cm) tall

DIRECTIONS

BODY

Make a loop with tail end of yarn on right, keeping ball end on left. Pull the ball end through loop.
Make one chain through loop on hook you have drawn through to steady the circle. Work 5 sc in to the circle and complete the circle with Sl st in to the first sc.

Body

Rnd 1: Sc 2 into each 5 sc.
Rnd 2: * Sc 1, 2 sc into next sc * five times.
Rnd 3: * Sc 2, 2 sc into next sc, * five times.
Rnds 4–10: Sc 1 all around.
Rnd 11: * Sc 2, skip 1, sc 1* five times.
Add the stuffing at this point.
Rnd 12: * Sc 1, skip 1, sc 1 * five times.
Rnd 13: * Sc 1, skip 1 * five times.
Fasten off.

NOSE

Make a loop as you did for the body, and 5 sc in to the circle.
Rnd 1: Sc 2 into each 5 sc.
Rnds 2–3: Sc 1 all around.
Fasten off.

EARS (MAKE TWO)

Make 18 chains, join the first chain and the last chain with Sl st, to form the circle.
Sc 15 all around the circle. Fasten off.

FINISHING — sew together following the diagram

Ears
Make single crochet stitches around the chain.

Felt ears
Sew felt shapes to the back of the chain ears.

Features
Sew on the nose and make cheeks out of felt.

Skinny sleepy cat

MATERIALS

C-2 (2.75 mm) hook
White angora
Light gray yarn (for muzzle, ears, legs,
and arms)
Red embroidery floss (for mouth)
Brown embroidery floss (for eyes)

MEASUREMENTS

4 in. (10 cm) tall

DIRECTIONS

BODY

Make a loop with tail end of yarn on right, keeping ball
end on left. Pull the ball end through loop.
Make one chain through loop on hook you have drawn
through to steady the circle. Work 5 sc in to the circle
and complete the circle with Sl st in to the first sc.
Rnd 1: Sc 2 into each of 5 sc.
Rnd 2: * Sc 1, 2 sc into next sc * five times.
Rnd 3: * Sc 2, 2 sc into next sc * five times.
Rnds 4–10: Sc 1 all around.
Rnd 11: * Sc 2, skip 1 * five times.
Rnd 12: Sc 1 all around.
Rnds 13–14: * Sc 1, skip 1 * five times.
Fasten off.

HEAD

Make a loop as before and 5 sc into the circle to start.
Rnd 1: Sc 2 into each 5 sc.
Rnd 2: * Sc 1, 2 sc into next sc * five times.
Rnd 3: * Sc 2, 2 sc into next sc * five times.
Rnd 4: * Sc 3, 2 sc into next sc * five times.
Rnds 5–9: Sc 1 all around.
Rnd 10: * Sc 3, skip 1 * five times.
Rnd 11: * Sc 2, skip 1 * five times.
    Add stuffing at this point.
Rnd 12: * Sc 1, skip 1 * five times.
Rnd 13: * Sc 1, skip 1 * five times.
Fasten off.

Body

Head

EARS (MAKE TWO)

With light gray yarn, ch 4.

Row 1: Ch 1, sc 1 to end.

Row 2: Sc 1 into next 3 st.

Row 3: Sc 1 into next 2 st.

Fasten off.

MUZZLE

With light brown yarn, make a loop as before and sc 5 into the circle to start.

Rnd 1: Sc 2 into each of 5 sc.

Rnd 2: * Sc 1, 2 sc into next sc * five times.

Fasten off.

Muzzle

Ears

ARMS AND LEGS (MAKE FOUR)

Make a loop as before and 5 sc into the circle to start.

Rnd 1: Sc 2 into each st.

Rnds 2–6: Sc 1 all around.

Rnd 7: * Sc 1, skip 1 * five times.

Fasten off; no need to stuff.

Arms / legs

Yawn!!
Time for a
catnap.

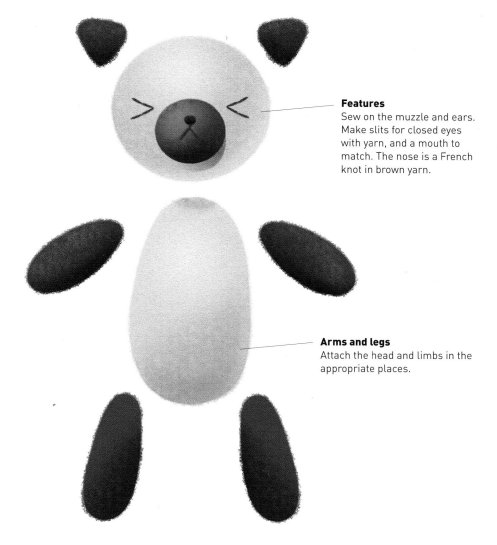

Features
Sew on the muzzle and ears. Make slits for closed eyes with yarn, and a mouth to match. The nose is a French knot in brown yarn.

Arms and legs
Attach the head and limbs in the appropriate places.

Skinny sleepy cat

Elephant

MATERIALS

E-4 (3.5 mm) hook
Blue yarn
Red embroidery floss (for mouth)
Plastic eyes ¼ in. (7 mm) diameter

MEASUREMENTS

4 in. (10 cm) tall

DIRECTIONS

BODY

Make a loop with tail end of yarn on right, keeping ball end on left. Pull the ball end through loop. Make one chain through loop on hook you have drawn through to steady the circle. Work 5 sc in to the circle and complete the circle with Sl st in the first sc.

Rnd 1: Sc 2 into each of 5 sc.
Rnd 2: * Sc 1, 2 sc into next sc * five times.
Rnd 3: * Sc 2, 2 sc into next sc * five times.
Rnd 4: * Sc 3, 2 sc into next sc * five times.
Rnds 5–9: Sc 1 all around.
Rnd 10: * Sc 3, skip 1 * five times.
Rnd 11: * Sc 2, skip 1 * five times.
　　　　Add the stuffing at this point.
Rnd 12: * Sc 1, skip 1 st, 1 sc * five times.
Rnd 13: * Sc 1, skip 1 st, * five times.
Fasten off.

HEAD

Make a loop as before and 5 sc into the circle to start.

Rnd 1: Sc 2 into each of 5 sc.
Rnd 2: * Sc 1, 2 sc into next sc * five times.
Rnd 3: * Sc 2, 2 sc into next sc * five times.
Rnd 4: * Sc 3, 2 sc into next sc * five times.
Rnds 5–9: Sc 1 all around.
Rnd 10: * Sc 3, skip 1 st, 1 sc * five times.
Rnd 11: * Sc 2, skip 1 st, 1 sc * five times.
　　　　Add the stuffing at this point.
Rnd 12: * Sc 1, skip 1 * five times.
Rnd 13: * Sc 1, skip 1 * five times.
Rnds 14–20: Sc 1 all around (for trunk).

Body

Head

EARS (MAKE TWO)

Make a loop as before and sc 5 into the circle to start.

Rnd 1: Sc 2 into each of 5 sc.

Rnd 2: * Sc 1, 2 sc into next sc * five times.

Rnd 3: * Sc 2, 2 sc into next sc * five times.

Fasten off.

ARMS (MAKE TWO)

Make a loop as before and sc 5 into the circle to start.

Rnd 1: Sc 2 into each st.

Rnd 2: * Sc 1, 2 sc into next sc * five times.

Rnds 3–4: Sc 1 all around.

Rnd 5: * Sc 1, skip 1, * five times.

Rnds 6–7: Sc 1 all around.

Rnd 8: * Sc 1, skip 1 * five times.

*Fasten off. No need to stuff.

LEGS (MAKE TWO)

Make a loop as before and 5 sc into the circle to start.

Rnd 1: Sc 2 into each st.

Rnd 2: * Sc 1, 2 sc into next sc * five times.

Rnds 3–7: Sc 1 all around.

Add stuffing, and fasten off.

× × × × × × × × × × × × × × × × 3 - 7

Legs

Ears

8
6, 7
5
3 - 4

Arms

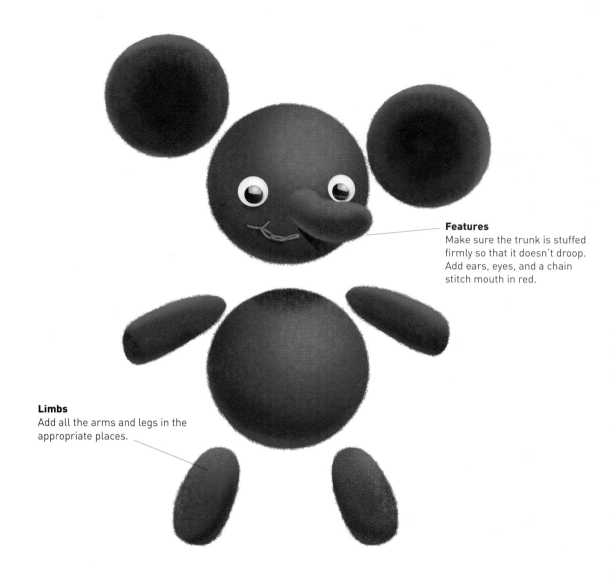

Features
Make sure the trunk is stuffed firmly so that it doesn't droop. Add ears, eyes, and a chain stitch mouth in red.

Limbs
Add all the arms and legs in the appropriate places.

Let's play

Amigurumi Gallery

THERE ARE AS MANY DIFFERENT STYLES OF AMIGURUMI AS THERE ARE MAKERS.

The Internet has served to make the crafting world ever smaller, and more fertile, keeping new ideas traveling, and growing, fast. It also works as a support network, with makers able to gain feedback on their work, as well as selling their wares to a wide audience. Group sites mean small crafters can afford to make a blog, or display their work in a way that would have been impossible a few years ago.

The increased use of diagrams and charts also means that patterns are translated more easily than in the past. Japanese craft books have a different aesthetic to work you can see in America or Europe. Their clear and novel style is sought-after in the West, and buying Japanese craft books has become the latest expensive pastime for serious crafters. Try searching for amigurumi on the web: here is a small selection of makers that we liked the look of.

Name: Niji aka Irisgurumi
Website: www.irisgurumi.com
A little about me... My name is Niji, I'm Thai, originally from Bangkok. Now I'm living in Alicante, Spain. In February 2007 I started my very first amigurumi – I had never touched a crochet hook before. Now, I can say that I love amigurumi.

Name: Cynthia Rae
Website: www.candypopcreations.etsy.com
A little about me... Working in Iowa, USA, Cynthia Rae is a textile artist in a permanent state of inspiration, designing original patterns that bring a unique, contemporary flair to classic fiber art.

Name: MUFFA aka Mariella's Unusual Fantasy Funny Animals
Website: www.muffa.bravehost.com
A little about me... I live in sunny Italy and love to create miniature animals. My mother and grandmother taught me to knit, crochet and embroider and I have been doing crafts ever since!
I have a passion for all things small, mini, micro and sweet. I surprise myself "giving life" to micro animals, bears, and fairies.
I usually work with a 0.50 mm hook – someday I'll go blind!

Name: Emily Miller aka Crochet Obsession
Website: www.crochetobsession.blogspot.com
A little about me... I live in Phoenix, Arizona, USA, with my husband and two children. I have been crocheting since I was 12, and for a long time I only made blankets. A combination of Mr Rogers, and my four-year-old got me back into crocheting after a long pause. Mr Rogers had a show where he visited a friend that made animals: my son loved the idea of having me make him an animal. What child wouldn't want their very own live-in toy maker? So my crochet obsession was reborn.

Name: Marci Senders
Website: www.marcisenders.com
A little about me... I am a Senior Designer for Random House Books for Young Readers. Other than crocheting in my spare time, I like to illustrate, collage and alter books.

Name: Samantha Wilson
Website: www.eureekaswindow.etsy.com
A little about me... A college student in Connecticut, USA, with an addiction to crafts, especially crocheting and sewing, I create my own amigurumi patterns based on random inspirations and things that I love.

Name: Ruby Submarine
Website: www.rubysubmarine. blogspot.com
A little about me... I currently live in Culver City, California, USA, I have been crafting since my grandmother taught me to knit when I was four. I am self-taught at crochet, have no idea how to use patterns and free-form crochet everything I make. My favourite things to make are sea creatures, hats and fake food (especially good for fake food fights).

Name: Hansigurumi aka Hansi Singh
Website: www.hansigurumi.etsy.com
A little about me... Hansigurumi, who is merely Hansi in her everyday life, credits her son Ambrose for inspiring a love of knitted toys and other peculiarities. She lives with Ambrose and her partner Aaron in Seattle, Washington, USA.

Name: Jenifer Spangenberg aka Truly Outrageous
Website: www.TrulyOutrageous.etsy.com
A little about me... I am from Cherry Hill, New Jersey, USA.

Name: Ana Paula Rimoli
Website: www.anapaulaoli.etsy.com
A little about me... Hola! My children
are the inspiration for all the toys
I make. I love, love, love crocheting
and making toys. I've been making
stuff for as long as I can remember
and I have to thank my neighbour
Martita in Montevideo for teaching
me how to crochet when I was little,
I think six or seven, sitting outside
one summer.

Name: My4heads aka Paulette Morrissey
Website: www.13sites.com
A little about me... Born and raised in Wisconsin, USA
– by day, I'm an artist, working in coloured pencils,
watercolours and ink. In the evenings, I like designing
little crochet creatures and patterns.

Name: Donielle Martin aka turtle kisses
Website: www.turtlekisses.com
A little about me... Donielle is a wife
and mother of three living in Minnesota,
USA, currently working as security for a
clothing store, but greatly enjoys making
amigurumi in her spare time.

Name: PlanetJune aka June Gilbank
Website: www.planetjune.com
A little about me... June designs original
crochet patterns for cute amigurumi
softies, and runs the PlanetJune craft
blog from Ontario, Canada.

Name: Leanne Poon aka t0fugurl
Website: www.t0fugurl.etsy.com
A little about me... I live in Vancouver, Canada, and I only started crocheting last summer. I had a preconception that crocheting was so "grandma", but I'm glad I learned how to make amigurumi and I've been hooked ever since.

Name: Eternal Sunshine aka Alicia Kachmar
Website: www.aliciakachmar.com
A little about me... I originally hail from Pittsburgh, PA, but currently live in Brooklyn, NY, USA. I'm a Jill-of-all-trades so to speak: a museum educator/teacher turned freelance writer/crafter/DIYer, and I love to cook and bake, bike-ride and explore.

Name: Jenni Love
Website: www.theselovinghands.etsy.com
A little about me... Living in Ontario, Canada, I am a mother of two wonderful boys. After crocheting for ten years, my sister introduced me to amigurumi and I got hooked. I now crochet my own original creatures and write patterns.

Name: Shelley Becking
Website: www.thehookery.etsy.com
A little about me... I live in Ottawa, Ontario, Canada. I took up crochet about a year ago while on maternity leave from my full-time job. My children and their imagination inspire most of my projects. I started to crochet My Pet Monster for my three-year-old and now I can't stop! I never know what Monster will be born until I'm done. They are OOAK (one of a kind).

Name: Wren Yu aka love yu critters
Website: www.loveyu.etsy.com
A little about me... I am a self-taught crafter who lives, loves, and crochets in Atlanta, Georgia, USA.

Name: Nelly Pailloux aka La Fée Crochette
Website: www.lafeecrochette.blogspot.com
A little about me... I'm French and totally addicted to creating tiny little creatures in my small workshop in the English countryside. I find inspiration in cookbooks and children's illustrations.

Name: Andrea Onishi aka Lacrafi
Website: www.lacrafiteira.etsy.com
www.superziper.blogspot.com (my craft
blog in Portuguese)
A little about me... I craft at my small
studio in São Paulo, Brazil. I crochet,
knit, sew and draw. My creative name
is Lacrafi (short for Lacrafiteira.) I love
making amigurumi because it is one
of the most creative handicrafts. With
pieces of yarn and crochet needles I feel
free to create the most amazing objects.

Name: Trinlay Khadro

Website: www.trinlayk.etsy.com

A little about me... I'm a long-time artist and crafter making my art and crafting my "real job", while learning how to live with illness and disability. I live with my almost grown-up daughter and two cats. I've discovered Etsy via Flickr, and hope it will be as much fun as it looks.

Name: Erin Nicholson aka squirrel of snooze
Website: www. squirrelofsnooze.etsy.com
A little about me...
Erin Nicholson is a Vancouver-based designer and artist, who would likely have never taken up crochet had it not been for the recent crafts revival and crafting community online.

Name: Julie King aka Gleefulthings
Website: www.gleefulthings.com
A little about me... I'm 24 and live in southern California. I have always loved making things! I learned how to crochet about three years ago and have been addicted ever since. About a year ago, I started my business Gleeful Things as a place to sell crocheted toys that I design, as well as crochet patterns that I've written.

Name: Amy Lin
Website: www.melbangel.etsy.com
A little about me... I am a stay-at-home mum from Singapore. I started crafting as a hobby. Then I found the Etsy site for handmade products. I became an online seller there. I mainly sell crochet patterns, which are all my original creations, and also some unique crocheted finished products. My customers come from many countries including the USA, UK, Australia, Malaysia, France, Sweden, and Thailand.

Name: Amy Gaines
Website: www.amygaines.etsy.com
A little about me... I am a stay-at-home mother, living in Massachusetts, USA, from where I operate my online pattern shop.

Name: Kim Yeoh
Website: www.kqcreative.com
A little about me... I am a handicraft hobbyist living in Singapore.

Name: Crochet Accessory
Website: www.crochetaccessory.com
A little about us... We are two sisters, both professional business women – one based in Shanghai and the other in New York – who share a fondness for unique crocheted artworks, especially amigurumi. We started our business of making and selling amigurumi about two years ago and hope to share our passion for amigurumi with a broader audience.

Name: Michelle
Website: www.chezmichelle.etsy.com
www.stores.ebay.com/Suncatchers-Eyes
A little about me... I started out designing crochet patterns – meet Little Emo – now my business has switched gears. I could never find the colours and sizes of acrylic safety eyes that I wanted, so I started painting my own. Now I sell Suncatcher Eyes on Etsy and eBay.

Name: Kim Werker
Website: www.kimwerker.com
A little about me... I am the editor of *Interweave Crochet* magazine and the founder of CrochetMe.com; I live in Vancouver, BC, Canada.

Name: Helena Shimizu aka kawaiikewpie
Website: www.kawaiikewpie.com
A little about me... I am a production artist working in a marketing agency in Los Angeles. During my freetime I enjoy handicrafts like amigurumi, drawing, and sewing by hand. I also collect, swap, and sell anything kawaii, Japanese for cute.

Name: Raewa dolly
Website: www.raewadolly.etsy.com
A little about me... Hello from Bangkok, Thailand. My sister and I love dolls. So, we thought that there are many people (not only kids) that love dolls and want to have a good collection of them – that's why we started RaewaDolly. You will see lots of dolls and cute stuff in our shop.

Name: Yuka Yamaguchi
Website: www.plastiquemonkey.com
A little about me... I was born in Kobe, Japan and am now living in Saskatoon, Canada. I've recently started telling people I'm an artist. I'm self-taught. I make useless toys and art for adult children. My ongoing project is the "turn everything around you cute and fun project."

Resources

The joy of knitting small is that you don't always need to rush out and buy a load of expensive yarn. However, should your amigurumi habit get out of hand, there are plenty of retailers that can help. Here are a few tried and tested suppliers that you can find on the internet and probably in your local yarn shop.

YARNS

Berroco, Inc.
14 Elmdale Rd.
PO Box 367
Uxbridge, MA 01569
info@berroco.com
www.berroco.com

Blue Sky Alpacas, Inc
PO Box 88
Cedar, MN 55011
www.blueskyalpacas.com

Brown Sheep Yarn Company
10062 County Road 16
Mitchell, NE 69357

Crystal Palace yarns
160 23rd St
Richmond, CA 94804
www.straw.com

Joann.com
2361 Rosecrans Ave
El Segundo, CA 90245

**Debbie Bliss, Rowan Yarns
distributed by Knitting Fever, Inc.
Knitting Fever, Inc.**
PO Box 502
Roosevelt, NY 11575
www.knittingfever.com

Koigu Wool Designs
RR #1
Williamsford, ON N0H 2V0
Canada
www.koigu.com

Lion Brand Yarns
135 Kero Road
Carlstadt, NJ 07072
www.lionbrand.com

Manos del Uruguay
www.rosiesyarncellar.com

Misti Alpaca
P.O.Box 2532
Glen Ellyn, Illinois, 60138
www.mistialpaca.com

GGH
distributed by Muench Yarns
285 Bel Marin Keys Blvd
Novata, CA 94949
www.muenchyarns.com

Patons
320 Livingstone Avenue South
Listowel, ON
N4W 3H3, Canada
www.patonsyarns.com

Plymouth Yarn Co.
PO Box 28
Bristol, PA 19007
pyc@plymouthyarn.com
www.plymouthyarn.com

HOOKS

Brittany
Post Office Box 130
Elk, California
www.brittanyneedles.com

Clover
www.clover-usa.com

Pony
www.pony-needles.com

Turn of the Century
1676 Millsboro Road
Mansfield, OH 44906-3374
www.turn2001

Right: You will never guess who these intrepid robbers are. They have made a haul and are making good their escape.

Index

A

amigurumi:
  development **11**
  meaning **9**
  sound of word **8**
Ana Paula **111**
animals: **111**
  balance **32**
  body shapes **32**
  designing **32–43**
  inspiration **32**
  positions **32**
  simplifying shapes **36–7**
  sketches **33–5**

B

balance **32**
Bear **34, 58–61**
Grumpy tiny mohair bear **62–5**
Becking, Shelley **115**
blanket stitch **38, 39**

C

cat, Skinny sleepy
Cat chain: **96–9**
  counting **23**
  making **23**
chain ring, making **24**
chain stitch **38, 39**
charts **9–10**
reading **16, 20–1, 29**
Cheeky Bunny **34, 50–3**
circular crochet **24**
making shapes with
crochet: **36–7**
  finishing off **28–9**
  techniques **22-9**
Crochet Accessory **122**
crochet hooks **18**
holding **22**
Crochet Obsession
  (aka Emily Miller) **108**
cubes, creating **37**

D

daruma dolls **12**
decreasing **16**
designing: **32–43**
  finishing touches **38–43**
  from sketches **32–5**
  inspiration **32**
  making shapes **36–7**
disc, flat **36**
dog, Sausage Dog
dolls: **78–81**
  Japanese **12–13**
  making **16**
Doll's Festival **13**
double crochet (dc) **26**

E

egg shape, creating **37**
Elephant **100–3**
embroidery stitches **38, 39**
ends, weaving in **29**
Eternal Sunshine
  (aka Alicia Kachmar) **114**
expressions **40–3**
eye lids **42**
eyebrows **43**
eyes **42–3, 48**

F

faces:
  expressions **40–3**
  positioning features in **41**
fastening off **29**
felt, sewing on **38, 49**
Field mouse **94–5**
finishing off **28–9**
finishing touches **38–43**

G

Gaines, Amy **121**
gallery **105–23**

gauge **16**
gift box, sketches **34**
gifts **12**
Gilbank, June
  (aka PlanetJune) **113**
Gleefulthings
  (aka Julie King) **120**
Grumpy tiny mohair bear **62–5**

H

hakata dolls **13**
half sphere, creating **37**
half-double crochet **26**
Hansigurumi
  (aka Hansi Singh) **110**
Hello Kitty **10**
Hina Matsuri dolls **13**
hooks **18**
holding **22**

I

increasing **16**
Irisgurumi (aka Niji) **106**

J

Japan **9–10**
Japanese dolls **12–13**

K

Kachmar, Alicia
  (aka Eternal Sunshine) **114**
kakeshi dolls **12**
karoshi **10**
kawaii **10**
Khadro, Trinlay **118**
King, Julie
  (aka Gleefulthings) **120**
knitters' pins **19**
knitting **9**

L

La Fée Crochette
   (aka Nelly Pailloux) **116**
Lacrafi (aka Andrea Onishi) **117**
Lin, Amy **121**
Lion **70–3**
Love, Jenni **115**
love yu critters (aka Wren Yu) **116**

M

magic ring, making **24**
Magpies **74–7**
Mariella's Unusual Fantasy
   Funny Animals
   (aka MUFFA) **107**
Martin, Donielle
   (aka turtle kisses) **112**
materials **18–19**
Michelle **122**
Miller, Emily
   (aka Crochet Obsession) **108**
momiji dolls **12**
Monkey **86–9**
Morrissey, Paulette
   (aka My4heads) **111**
mouse, Field mouse **94–5**
MUFFA (Mariella's Unusual
   Fantasy Funny Animals) **107**
muzzles **40**
My4heads
   (aka Paulette Morrissey) **111**

N

needles **19**
Nicholson, Erin
   (aka squirrel of snooze) **119**
Niji (aka Irisgurumi) **106**

O

okiagari-koboshi dolls **12**
omiyage **12**

Onishi, Andrea (aka Lacrafi) **117**
Owl **35, 82–5**

P

Pailloux, Nelly
   (aka La Fée Crochette) **116**
Panda Bear **90–3**
patterns: **9–10**
   reading charts **16, 20–1, 29**
Penguins **54–7**
Pig **46–9**
pins **19**
PlanetJune
   (aka June Gilbank) **113**
plastic pellets **16**
Poon, Leanne (aka t0fuguri) **114**

R

Rabbit **33**
Cheeky Bunny **34, 50–3**
Rae, Cynthia **106**
Raewa dolly **123**
resources **124–5**
Rimoli, Ana Paula **111**
round, working in **24**

S

satin stitch **38, 39**
Sausage Dog **78–81**
sausage shape, creating **37**
scissors **19**
Senders, Marci **108**
Shimizu, Helena **123**
Singh, Hansi
   (aka Hansigurumi) **110**
single crochet join **29**
single crochet (sc) **25**
sketches **32**
Skinny sleepy Cat **96–9**
slip stitch, making **23**
slip stitch join **29**
slipknot **22**

Spangenberg, Jenifer
   (aka Truly Outrageous) **110**
sphere: **36–37**
   creating **36**
   half, creating **37**
spirals, working in **16**
squares, creating **37**
squirrel of snooze
   (aka Erin Nicholson) **119**
stitch markers **16, 19, 36**
stitches:
   crochet **22–7**
   embroidery **38, 39**
stuffing **16**
Submarine, Ruby **109**

T

t0fuguri (aka Leanne Poon) **114**
Tanuki (racoon dog) **33, 66–9**
tape measure **19**
techniques **22–9**
treble crochet (tc) **27**
Truly Outrageous
   (aka Jenifer Spangenberg) **110**
turtle kisses
   (aka Donielle Martin) **112**

W

weaving in ends **29**
weight, adding **16**
Werker, Kim **123**
whipstitch **29, 39**
Wilson, Samantha **109**

Y

Yamaguchi, Yuka **123**
yarns: **16, 18**
   experimenting with **32**
   holding **22**
   new, joining in **36**
Yeoh, Kim **121**
Yu, Wren (aka love yu critters) **116**